COMMUNICATION-FOCUSED THERAPY (CFT) – SPECIFIC DIAGNOSES (VOL II)

2nd Edition

Christian Jonathan

Haverkampf MD

PPC

Psychiatry Psychotherapy Communication
Publishing Ltd

COMMUNICATION-FOCUSED THERAPY (CFT) – SPECIFIC DIAGNOSES

Psychiatry Psychotherapy Communication
Publishing Ltd

Published by Psychiatry Psychotherapy Communication
Publishing Ltd
Dublin

First published in the United States of America by
Psychiatry Psychotherapy Communication
Publishing Ltd
San Francisco, CA, USA

Printed in the United States of America
Set in Calibri

Table of Contents

Introduction 1

Attention Deficit Hyperactivity Disorder (ADHD) 3

Adjustment Disorder 15

Autism and Asperger Syndrome 35

Bipolar Disorder 42

Borderline Personality Disorder (BPD) 51

Burnout 61

Depression 70

Eating Disorders 78

Narcissism 87

Obsessive-Compulsive Disorder (OCD) 93

Paranoia 97

Psychosis 105

Posttraumatic Stress Disorder (PTSD) 114

Schizophrenia 123

Sexual Disorders 129

Social Anxiety and Shyness 138

Psychotherapeutic Technique: A Brief Overview 148

References 161

Introduction

Communication-Focused Therapy (CFT) was developed by the author to focus more specifically on the communication process between patient and therapist. (Haverkampf, 2017d) The central piece is that the sending and receiving of meaningful messages is at the heart of any change process. CBT, psychodynamic psychotherapy and IPT help because they define a format in which communication processes take place that can bring about change. However, CBT, and to a lesser extent psychodynamic psychotherapy, do not work directly with the communication processes. (Haverkampf, 2017c) CFT attempts to do so.

We engage constantly in communication. The cells in our bodies do so with each other using electrical current, molecules, vibrations or even electromagnetic waves. People communicate with each other also through a multitude of channels, which may on several technologies and intermediaries. It does not have to be an email. Spoken communication requires multiple signal translations from electrical and chemical transmission in the nervous system to mechanical transmission as the muscles and the air stream determine the motions of the vocal chords and then as sound waves travelling through the air, followed by various translations on the receiving end. At each end, in the sender and in the receiver, there is also a processing of information which relies on the highly complex networks of the nervous system. Communication, in short, happens everywhere all the time. It is an integral part of life. Certain communication patterns can, however, also contribute to experiencing anxiety and panic attacks.

Autoregulation

Communication is an autoregulatory mechanism. It ensures that living organisms, including people, can adapt to their environment and live a life according to their interests, desires, values, and aspirations. This does not only require communicating with a salesperson, writing an exam paper or watching a movie, but also finding out more about oneself, psychologically and physically. Whether measuring one's strength at the gym or engaging in self-talk, this self-exploration requires flows of relevant and meaningful information. Communication allows us to have a sense of self and a grasp of who we are and what we need and want in the world, but it has to be learned similar to our communication with other people.

A Change Process

Communication is not just autoregulative but also can lead to change with a view to the future.

Attention Deficit Hyperactivity Disorder (ADHD)

Introduction

Attention Deficit Hyperactivity Disorder (ADHD) can interfere significantly with a person's private and professional life. Often, there are already problems in school which cause low self-confidence and prevent a healthy belief in one's resources and talents before they can even be tested. Difficulties concentrating and focusing on the work at hand can be so severe to make school work, or later performance in one's job, close to impossible. This can cause huge suffering, as both the individual afflicted with ADHD and his or her family and close friends often have to watch helplessly as one failure follows another.

On the other hand, this does not have to be the case. Medication is usually very effective in treating the symptoms of ADHD. The most common type of medication are the stimulants. (Haverkampf, 2018) However, this should in most cases be accompanied by a course of psychotherapy to help with the problems resulting from the ADHD und to treat the ADHD itself. Treatment with stimulants has been shown to be effective for over a year, while its long-term effectiveness is unclear. Even without treatment, adolescents and adults tend to develop coping skills which make up for some or all of their impairments.

Communication Patterns

ADHD has a lot to do with how one interacts with the environment. Strategies, which maybe worked for a while, are not as helpful anymore. In therapy, in the interaction between therapist and patient new communication patterns can be developed. ADHD is a condition which leads to an alteration in how individuals communicate with their environment and it leads to problems with the environment. Patients have greater difficulties to filter out relevant information from the stream of information reaching them. (Haverkampf, 2017b) Medication can help significantly to help the patients focus on a particular stream of communication, while psychotherapy should help to consciously select the information and the interactions that are meaningful and relevant to the individual. (Haverkampf, 2017e)

Understanding Communication

Understanding how communication works can be very helpful to a patient suffering from ADHD. This means not just explaining how messages and meaning are sent and received, but also to allow the patient to experiment in the therapeutic setting. This should be the space where the patient feels safe and supported enough to engage in experimenting with communication which in the long-run is effective in dealing with the ADHD itself as well as the secondary communication and relationship effects. The more a patient understands how meaning and relationships are created and maintained in relevant and effective communication, the more of a sense of control he or she will have. For a child it may also be helpful to demonstrate and experiment with the explanation in a playful way. This also helps strengthen the therapeutic relationship and motivate towards therapy.

Understanding communication begins with becoming more aware of interactions and developing a habit to reflect on them and one's own thoughts while having them (metacognition). The therapeutic interaction between therapist and patient helps the patient practice and become more competent at it. The therapist provides feedback on the interaction and explains some of the key mechanisms of communication. For a patient with ADHD, the latter may include explanations on how boundaries work, differences between empathy and sympathy, how focus is and can be influenced, how internal communication works where the sources of relevant information are inside the patient and not in the environment, and how the patient can reconnect and use internal information to identify what is relevant and meaningful to him.

Attention Deficit Hyperactivity Disorder (ADHD)

Attention deficit hyperactivity disorder (ADHD) is a mental disorder of the neurodevelopmental type. It is characterized by problems paying attention, excessive activity, or difficulty controlling behavior which is not appropriate for a person's age. The symptoms appear before a person is twelve years old, are present for more than six months, and cause problems in at least two settings (such as school, home, or recreational activities). In children, problems paying attention may result in poor school performance. Although it causes impairment, particularly in modern society, many children with ADHD have a good attention span for tasks they find interesting. Its causes are unknown.

It is thus not a condition which interferes with the ability to focus and concentrate globally, but one that makes it important to help patients see enjoyment and meaning in everyday tasks. If something feels relevant, patients with ADHD often have less of a problem with it. The important task is to help the patient identify relevance in things and focus increasingly on thoughts, activities and objects of increasing relevance. This, however, requires a better connection with oneself and greater awareness for the communication from within oneself. Aside from the important work in therapy, several approaches, such as body work (e.g. yoga) and meditation can be helpful. Rather than a withdrawal from oneself, however, greater sensitivity and perceptiveness vis-à-vis oneself is needed. In the therapeutic session the focus needs to be on what the patient values, needs, wishes and aspires to. (Haverkampf, 2017a, 2017b, 2017f)

Cutting Through Complexity

The interaction in the therapy session should help the patient build a concept of herself and the world, which also supports her in pursuing her needs, values and aspirations. Humans use strategies to communicate, which are again the result of pas communication experiences and the thoughts and emotions they elicited and are associated with. In ADHD, patients are often desperate because they cannot interact with their environment to the extent they would like to, which to a certain extent also applies to the interactions they are having with themselves. The neurobiological divergence from the 'norm' in ADHD means strategies that might work for others do not work as well for someone who is suffering from ADHD. While medication can make strategies people not suffering from ADHD use for interpersonal interactions and work or study more effective, another approach is to develop strategies that work for the individual suffering from ADHD. Since the exchange of information plays a significant role in life, a special role falls to the communication strategies.

The Uniquely Special in the Complex

One way to see more meaning and relevance in tasks is to know more about them. Knowing more about a task makes connections between tasks and own interests and aspirations clearer. For example, schoolwork as an end in itself may not be very motivating, not just to people suffering from ADHD. However, if a subject matter can be closely linked to a value or a need, it becomes more relevant, more meaningful and more motivating.

For most people it is not motivating to do things, just because one does them, but this is especially true for someone with ADHD. There has to be an emotional reason to engage in it. People without ADHD have may find it easier to postpone gratification into the future but engaging in a task in the long-run which is not very meaningful to oneself leads to dissatisfaction in anyone. One may say that individuals with ADHD are more sensitive to that, which is not a bad thing in itself, but it requires paying particular attention to it. Unfortunately, many individuals with ADHD feel they have to change themselves, rather than the strategies they are using and their environment. Discussing this aspect in therapy can also relieve some unneeded pressure.

Acting on Values, Interests and Aspirations

The therapeutic interactions should illustrate to the patient and convey the sense of competence and confidence that communication is a powerful tool to get one's needs and aspirations met. An important part of the process is that the patient can gradual take over increasing responsibility for the therapeutic interactions and feel a greater sense of efficacy and influence over the process dynamics.

Giving patients with ADHD a greater sense of being in control of their own destiny and interacting with others and shaping the world in a way which gets their needs and wants met. Even though young patients with ADHD seem demanding and in control of things in a wild way, at the core they are very conscious of not being in control over events in life. There is the constant sense of not getting what one needs and wants, especially in older patients, which leads to misdiagnoses of personality disorders, particularly narcissism or dissocial personality disorder. It is important to see the ADHD with its maladaptive communication patterns with oneself and others at the core.

Reconnection

In ADHD there is often a strong sense of disconnect. In the therapeutic settings the communication patterns can be used to discover meaning in things that are important to the patient as well as things in the outside world. This can make it easier to match up the one and the other.

Understanding ADHD

Someone suffering from ADHD can focus quite well on things that are motivating. However, for things that are not motivating it can be far more difficult to focus and concentrate on. Thus motivation, or seeing relevance and potential excitement and satisfaction, in things is probably more relevant to someone suffering from ADHD.

Many therapeutic approaches target the focus or concentration rather than motivation. However, changing motivation and making things more meaningful may be a better long-term strategy. This usually requires developing better communication techniques and strategies with oneself and others. However, the goal is not just communication in itself, but the skills for a better understanding of the world around and oneself. One of the problems in ADHD is that the world is not fuller but emptier. The hyperactivity and frequent switching of activities, interests and so on, prevents patients with ADHD from getting a deeper view for something, which also makes it more difficult to develop the motivation and initiative to stay with an activity. An effective way to resolve this dilemma is through communication, and by helping the patient to get more meaningful information from herself and her environment.

Disconnection

There is a vicious cycle in which the symptoms of ADHD cause a disconnectedness from oneself and others. This not only leads to feelings of loneliness, but also to a loss of a sense of effectiveness in the world, the ability to effect changes and to get ones needs, wants and aspirations met. The disconnect is often a result of the perceived failure in carrying out tasks which seem effortless to others, like schoolwork or otherwise simple repetitive tasks. Later in life, they can lead to resignation on the job and resentment towards others. Of course, at the core is anger, hopeless and helplessness about oneself. The antidote to this is the reconnection already mentioned above.

Motivation

There is usually a lot of motivation to change things in patients suffering from ADHD. Helplessness and hopelessness do their part to decrease the motivation even further. As we have already discussed, motivation and initiative to stay on an activity can be increased by perceiving and seeing more in it. However, motivation should also be addressed directly. For some time, there has been some discussion about a possible overlap between atypical depression and ADHD. While most therapists working in the field would agree that ADHD is a distinct and, particularly in severe cases, an easily distinguishable condition, negative thinking and a poor self-image are often as much a feature of ADHD as they are of most forms of depression. In ADHD, however, this often seems to be a consequence of the symptoms rather than being one of them. When individuals feel they cannot accomplish tasks others can or feel the world is overwhelming and stressful, as many individuals with ADHD feel, their self-image is bound to deteriorate. One way to get out of this, is reconnect with oneself by exploring in the therapy interests and values, as well as good past experiences and what made them feel good. By working through this with a pragmatic logic, empathy and openness, a patient can feel more grounded and develop a distance to overly stressful or painful situations in the present/

Meaning

In therapy an important part is to rediscover meaning and find it in the things that are relevant to the patient. Relevant is anything that is close to his or her values, basic interests, aspirations, wants, wishes and desires.

Seeing communications as meaningful requires perceiving a relevance to oneself in them, as well as a message that can bring about some change. In many situations it may be that it is difficult to spot meaningfulness in something before it has been tried out, but people often engage in it anyhow if they believe that it holds the potential to be meaningful. Much in the world would never have been accomplished without this course of action. To people suffering from ADHD, such a way of doing things seems to be closed off. The emotionally felt relevance and meaningfulness has to be there right away. So, an important question becomes how to bridge this gap in time. CFT aspires to do just this by working with meaningful messages in the exchange between therapist and patient.

Experiencing the World

Communication helps in identifying and finding meaning, either communication with oneself or with others. The exchange of messages is like a learning process in which meaning can be identified, found and accumulated. Through meaningful interactions one accumulates more meaning, more connectedness with oneself and the world and reduces the need for thoughts and behaviors which are triggered by fears, guilt, self-blame and other negative emotions. This also helps against depression and anxiety.

Perceiving more meaning also makes interacting with others and oneself more meaningful. This has a positive effect on one's interaction patterns, how and in which one ways one relates to one's environment and exchanges messages with it. The fact that meaning can be created in an interaction, or any instance of communication, can be liberating from someone with ADHD because it means one does not have to wait for meaning. It is already there, if one just engages in it.

Communication Patterns

The patterns in which people communicate determine the benefits the communication process. If the interaction patterns are not helpful in understanding messages from another or not helpful in reacting to the messages from others, they are not doing what they are supposed to do, or at least not fully. Then it is time to change them, which can be accomplished in the therapeutic setting, which not only provides feedback (to both, therapist and patient) and fertile ground for experimenting with new communication patterns, but also gives everyone participating in it the opportunity to feel how specific communication patterns feel.

In ADHD, the communication space of a therapeutic setting can help the patient to find more confidence and experience more authorship in affecting the dynamic, as well as develop insight into oneself and how to see more meaning in the world. The interaction with another human being can bring about the discovery of more meaning in the world. That is a basic axiom of communication theory and shows again and again in the practice of psychotherapy.

Values, Needs and Aspirations

Often, individuals suffering from ADHD have become uncertain about what is really important to them and the fit between these values and interests and their current life situation. Whether in the professional or romantic realms, getting what one needs and values makes happy in the long run, everything else does not. If I value helping people, it is important that I do that to make me happy. At the same time, I might value time spent with friend and spending time by myself. It is important that I can do this in the long run, because otherwise I will not be as happy as I could be.

To discover what is meaningful it is helpful to spend some effort on identifying values, needs and aspirations. This process can be very helpful to adults but may be more difficult in children and adolescents who are still developing and understanding of these parameters. Helpful here could be engaging in play or other activities where they can be identified. In adults this can be accomplished within a normal psychotherapy setting.

Meaningful Messages as the Instrument of Change

Communication is the vehicle of change. The instruments are meaningful messages which are generated and received by the people who take part in these interactions. In a therapeutic setting, keeping the mutual flow of information relevant and meaningful brings change in both people who take part in this process. The learning curve for the patient may be steeper in certain respects because he or she spends less time in this interaction style than a therapist.

Adjustment Disorder

Introduction

Life is about change. An organism has many ways to adjust to change and bring about internal and external change in return to accommodate the change. However, in a complex world people may not see anymore what change is appropriate and possible, this can then cause internal conflicts, which can cause psychiatric symptoms, such as in the form of anxiety or depression. Often, the feeling that something is out of sync between the own wishes, needs and values and the job or relationship one is in at the moment, may be there, but is suppressed out of a fear of change.

Communication makes change easier and breaks through the rigidity adjustment disorder often brings along. The messages and feedback one receives from others is screened for relevance before processing it further and effecting a change, which can help the individual to adapt better to the world around. Certain events, however, can be sudden and alter one's perception of the future. They may not seem as big to other people. What is important is how they are viewed by the individual.

A more meaningful communication with oneself and the environment can help reconnecting with the emotions that cause some of the symptoms the patient is experiencing. It can also help to make the world more meaningful again to the individual.

Adjustment Disorder

Adjustment disorder is an abnormal and excessive reaction to an identifiable life stressor. The reaction is more severe than would normally be expected and can result in significant impairment in social, occupational, or academic functioning. Symptoms must arise within three months of the onset of the stressor and last no longer than six months after the stressor has ended.

The response may be linked to a single event (a flood or fire, marriage, divorce, starting school, a new job) or multiple events (marital problems or severe business difficulties). Stressors may be recurrent events (a child witnessing parents constantly fighting, chemotherapy, financial difficulties) or continuous (living in a crime-ridden neighborhood).

Adjustment disorder often occurs with one or more of the following: depressed mood, anxiety, disturbance of conduct (in which the patient violates rights of others or major age-appropriate societal norms or rules), and maladaptive reactions (i.e. problems related to work or school, physical complaints, social isolation).

Adjustment disorders are associated with high risk of suicide and suicidal behavior, substance abuse, and the prolongation of other medical disorders or interference with their treatment. Adjustment disorder that persists may progress to become a more severe mental disorder, such as major depressive disorder.

Understanding Adjustment Disorder

Adjusting to changed circumstances or situations can be difficult. They can trigger a fear of the unknown, not just externally but also internally, an uneasiness about one's own motions. In the end, the fear of one's own emotions can often be the most difficult part. We know how we have felt in the past in a relationship, at a job, or with someone still alive, but we may be apprehensive about how this is going to be in the future after the change has happened.

Fear of Change

Life is constant change. This is important for survival and improvement. However, at the same time there is a need for some level of predictability to be able to make decisions. We need continuity in some respects to be able to weigh off different scenarios in the future. This is why there are laws, rules, science, and other areas of knowledge to help us make decisions. Internally, our values, basic interests and various feelings help us to make decisions that help us align decisions we make in the world with what we need and want. Knowing more about them establishes a greater sense of safety and consistency.

The fear of change is usually lower in people who know more about themselves and about the world. This reduces the fear of change and helps in making better decisions. How to get there is usually through communication. By having a better connection with oneself and the world around the level of meaningful information one has can be increased. But this often requires reducing the fear of communication, the anxiety of openness with oneself and others. Openness is important because communication is inherently a two-way street.

Communication Anxiety

Areas which people often feel anxious about are where there has been an issue with their interpersonal interactions in the past. Early traumata, like a disappearing or abusive parent, stay unresolved. For example, if a parent feels fearful and angry with himself and this is picked up by a child, the latter may decode these messages correctly in that the parent is angry, but since the parent may not be conscious about it, the child does not pick up on the second important half of the message, that the parent has a problem with himself and his issue is unrelated to the child. Of course, one can learn to pick up on the self-blame and frustration of the parent, and therapists should become experts at reading between the lines in this fashion, but it requires experience, reflection and insight into transference and counter-transference phenomena, for example, to use the psychoanalytic terms.

Fear of Own Emotions

Changes in life can change how individuals see themselves in the future. This is an unknown which is more anxiety provoking if one has a less stable sense of oneself. Basic needs, wants and values do not change much, and identifying them can return a greater sense of stability. One important objective of therapy is therefore to reduce the fear to make change possible.

Fears of Knowing the Self

One can feel oneself without describing it. One feels often oneself if one does things that are meaningful to oneself. Usually this comes with feelings of happiness or joy, while distancing oneself in one's actions and thoughts from oneself leads to uneasiness or negative feelings. One reason people often try to disconnect from or suppress their emotions is to feel themselves less. However, disconnecting from one's values and basic interests leads to bad feelings or a sense of emptiness. Overcoming one's anxiety of communicating with oneself, and also of communicating with others in a meaningful way, usually makes reconnecting much easier and almost automatic.

Meaning

Having to adjust to a new situation may mean that some meaningful people, things or activities are lost, while new ones have not been identified yet. In therapy an important part is to rediscover meaning and find it in the things that are relevant to the patient. Relevant is anything that is close to his or her values, basic interests, aspirations, wants, wishes and desires.

An important step in therapy thus to make the person aware of how anxiety affects one's thinking. Individuals from anxiety often focus differently from other individuals. There is often a focus on worst outcomes and strong fears which are caused by it. Underlying this are often strong emotions or conflicts which need to be defended against. The danger and uncertainty are quite frequently inside oneself, rather than on the outside. An individual with a fear of flying may be more afraid of not containing oneself and not being able to leave the plain than anything else. Anxiety is the fear of crashing oneself and the feelings of a dreaded uncertainty about oneself and one's emotional states.

Experiencing the World

If there has been change, the world has changed in a way. This can also mean that one has to adapt one's roles in various settings to the new situation. Being open to communication here can speed up the process of adapting to a changed world. It is through the interactions with others, that helpful and beneficial change can take place.

Values, Needs and Aspirations

Often, individuals suffering from anxiety or burnout have become uncertain about what is really important to them and the fit between these values and interests and their current life situation. Whether in the professional or romantic realms, getting what one needs and values makes happy in the long run, everything else does not. If I value helping people, it is important that I do that to make me happy. At the same time, I might value time spent with friend and spending time by myself. It is important that I can do this in the long run, because otherwise I will not be as happy as I could be.

Meaningful Messages as the Instrument of Change

Communication is the vehicle of change. The instruments are meaningful messages which are generated and received by the people who take part in these interactions. In a therapeutic setting, keeping the mutual flow of information relevant and meaningful brings change in both people who take part in this process. The learning curve for the patient may be steeper in certain respects because he or she spends less time in this interaction style than a therapist.

Anxiety and Panic Attacks

Introduction

Anxiety is like any other emotion a heightened mental state with a higher probability of certain conscious processes and behaviors. An individual suffering from anxiety dreads uncertain and often ill-defined events in the future or immediate future. The problem with anxiety is that the more one engages with it the more intense it becomes. However, anxiety can also be an important signal that something in life is 'out of sync'. It is important to treat an anxiety disorder, while also dealing with possible underlying issues to attain a long-term recovery.

Uncertainty

Anxiety requires a certain amount of uncertainty that is felt relevant by the individual. Life has its uncertainties, and this has to be accepted, but a person with an anxiety disorder focuses more on the uncertainty than others might. There can be a number of reasons for this, including past experiences where in a situation both uncertainty and emotional pain were felt, which the brain reinterpreted as uncertainty causing pain or hurt. But there may also be a heightened need for structure and certainty, which may to a certain extent also be biologically determined. But whatever the reason, acquiring a new perspective on uncertainty and feeling competency in using communication to reduce uncertainty, and thereby anxiety, usually reduces the anxiety levels significantly.

'Out of Sync'

Individuals often are more likely to encounter anxiety when there is an underlying feeling that something or things in their life are 'out of sync'. This can occur in many situations in professional or private realms. However, often it is uncertainty and when something in life is out of sync. The uncertainty can often be as a consequence of interpersonal difficulties which can arise in a relationship, at the work place or another area in life.

Life is 'out of sync' if it does not correlate anymore with one's values, basic interests, aspirations, true needs, wants and desires. Through one's behaviors and thoughts one finds out more about oneself, but one does not have to know these parameters consciously in order to have a sense for what is meaningful in one's life, which, however, requires being connected emotionally to one oneself in a meaningful way. Individuals who are suffering from burnout, for example, often experience this disconnect.

Panic Attacks

Panic attacks are intense phases of anxiety and can often occur 'out' of the blue. Still, in any case, exploring and looking into the panic attack can often unearth reasons for the panic attack. Panic attacks are sudden periods of intense fear that may include palpitations, sweating, shaking, shortness of breath, numbness, or a feeling that something bad is going to happen. The maximum degree of symptoms occurs within minutes. Typically, they last for about 30 minutes, but the duration can vary from seconds to hours. There may be a fear of losing control or chest pain. Panic attacks themselves are not dangerous physically.

Communication

Communication is the key to resolving anxiety and panic attacks. Often, it may be emotions which have not been resolved or addressed yet. Emotional conflicts and getting used to anxiety, can trigger and maintain it. Anxiety can mean being outside the social network, outside the web of communication which is the web of life, where autoregulatory processes help life adapt n new, and often also novel, ways.

However, since communication with oneself and others is also the process which makes the world a safer, more comfortable and interesting place, feeling more effective and competent in it, reduces anxiety. The communication process in the therapy sessions is important to create an understanding and insight in the patient for the importance of communication and to provide a safe space in which enquiry and experimentation is possible.

Uncertainty

Communication also helps bring more certainty in the world. The more confidence one has in oneself to communicate effectively, the safer one feels in life and the more certain it seems. Being able to deal with a certain amount of uncertainty s important to come up with novel answers and solutions to problems or to be creative in any meaningful way.

Psychodynamic Psychotherapy and CBT

Both of these therapies have shown effectiveness in the treatment of anxiety and panic attacks. Both have theories about why they help. The former sees learning processes about certain thought processes as central, the latter psychodynamic processes that bring about a change. However, they both neglect the communication process and changes in how people communicate as what ultimately helps. The difference to interpersonal psychotherapy is that the latter focuses more on the interpersonal setting than the actual communication processes.

Anxiety

Anxiety is an emotion characterized by an unpleasant state of inner turmoil, often accompanied by nervous behavior, such as pacing back and forth, somatic complaints, and rumination. It is the subjectively unpleasant feelings of dread over anticipated events, such as the feeling of imminent death. Anxiety is not the same as fear, which is a response to a real or perceived immediate threat, whereas anxiety is the expectation of future threat. Anxiety is a feeling of uneasiness and worry, usually generalized and unfocused as an overreaction to a situation that is only subjectively seen as menacing. It is often accompanied by muscular tension, restlessness, fatigue and problems in concentration. Anxiety can be appropriate, but when experienced regularly the individual may suffer from an anxiety disorder.

People facing anxiety may withdraw from situations which have provoked anxiety in the past. There are various types of anxiety. Existential anxiety can occur when a person faces angst, an existential crisis, or nihilistic feelings. People can also face mathematical anxiety, somatic anxiety, stage fright, or test anxiety. Social anxiety and stranger anxiety are caused when people are apprehensive around strangers or other people in general. Furthermore, anxiety has been linked with physical symptoms such as IBS and can heighten other mental health illnesses such as OCD and panic disorder.

Anxiety can be either a short term "state" or a long term "trait". Whereas trait anxiety represents worrying about future events, anxiety disorders are a group of mental disorders characterized by feelings of anxiety and fear. Anxiety disorders are partly genetic but may also be due to drug use, including alcohol, caffeine, and benzodiazepines (which are often prescribed to treat anxiety), as well as withdrawal from drugs of abuse. They often occur with other mental disorders, particularly bipolar disorder, eating disorders, major depressive disorder, or certain personality disorders.

Understanding Anxiety and Panic Attacks

Anxiety and Panic Attacks are related to how people communicate with themselves and with others. They often occur when a relationship breaks apart or some other interpersonal change or issue causes. The result is often communicative patterns that are maladaptive to the individual. These changes in communication patterns are what causes then the problems to the individuals.

Often, there are already maladaptive communication patterns before, that cause the problems in the relationship or interpersonal interactions. These patterns can be analyzed and changed. Another important element is that communication can also take place on the inside of the individual.

Uncertainty

In life, one has to live with uncertainty. Uncertainty just means that there is no manual in the beginning and there are still unknowns which leave room for excitement and exploration. Life is a learning experience. An individual suffering from anxiety may have areas in life where she thrives on excitement, and other areas where images of worst case scenarios cause her to freeze when she just considers a change in action or any action at all. Uncertainty to someone suffering from anxiety seems to be bearable in some areas and avoided in others. Often, the areas where it is not tolerated feel meaningful only to the person suffering from anxiety.

Communication Deficits

Areas which people often feel anxious about are where there has been an issue with their interpersonal interactions in the past. Early traumata, like a disappearing or abusive parent, stay unresolved. For example, if a parent feels fearful and angry with himself and this is picked up by a child, the latter may decode these messages correctly in that the parent is angry, but since the parent may not be conscious about it, the child does not pick up on the second important half of the message, that the parent has a problem with himself and his issue is unrelated to the child. Of course, one can learn to pick up on the self-blame and frustration of the parent, and therapists should become experts at reading between the lines in this fashion, but it requires experience, reflection and insight into transference and counter-transference phenomena, for example, to use the psychoanalytic terms.

Avoidance

Anxiety can lead to avoidance, which in turn can attach even more anxiety to the situations or behaviors which are being avoided. In social situations, not interacting with others deprives the person of continuously updating and honing the skills and confidence of interacting with others. Avoidance can thus lead to an increase rather than a decrease in anxiety in the long-run.

Reversing the Disconnect

Anxiety and panic attacks often are more about the uncertainty experienced inside oneself than about external events. The fear of flying, for example, is often more about the individual's internal emotional states than about the safety of the airplane. People with anxiety often fear more that they crash than that they airplane crashes.

To reverse the disconnect it is helpful to work as usual with the communication processes. Having the patient experience how communication can both be powerful in effectiveness and shaped according to the needs and desires of the patient, brings the patient back to developing more competence and trust in the own abilities to communicate.

When working with a patient suffering from anxiety, it is particularly important to help a patient in feeling that she is making herself understood. This requires reflecting often on the communication dynamics and on how the therapist and the patient understands and feels about the other person's message, and what the message may have meant to the person communicating it. In this process, therapist and patient become partners in an exploration of a dynamic, which is always different if one partner changes, whether the patient or the therapist. The therapist offers experience and skills, which prevent the two from getting lost. Over time, the patient acquires the necessary skills, insight and experience to do this on her own.

Looking Back

Connecting with oneself means using all the information that is available to find out more about oneself. Previous life experiences and how one felt and feels about them can be helpful. It does not mean going back into traumata or reliving something but finding what has been relevant and meaningful to oneself. From this one can gain insight into what is truly important to oneself. From there, it is usually quite easy to have some ideas about what to engage in more or less now and in the future.

Meaning

Individuals suffering from anxiety and panic attacks often see less meaning in the things they do. In therapy an important part is to rediscover meaning and find it in the things that are relevant to the patient. Relevant is anything that is close to his or her values, basic interests, aspirations, wants, wishes and desires.

Awareness of the Inner Workings of Anxiety

An important step in therapy thus to make the person aware of how anxiety affects one's thinking. Individuals from anxiety often focus differently from other individuals. There is often a focus on worst outcomes and strong fears which are caused by it. Underlying this are often strong emotions or conflicts which need to be defended against. The danger and uncertainty is quite frequently inside oneself, rather than on the outside. An individual with a fear of flying may be more afraid of not containing oneself and not being able to leave the plain than anything else. Anxiety is the fear of crashing oneself and the feelings of a dreaded uncertainty about oneself and one's emotional states.

This insight into the inner workings of anxiety is useful because it helps to formulate new strategies in interacting with oneself and with others.

Interacting with Oneself

Communication with oneself in itself should be viewed as meaningful. Especially if there is stress in the environment, such as in difficult situations in the workplace or in a relationship, there is a greater tendency to disconnect from oneself to reduce the pressure for change from the inside. However, it is often the information from the own feelings and thoughts which can provide more certainty and direction. Working out the own basic parameters, such as needs, values, aspirations, can help to formulate plans and strategies to resolve a situation. This requires, however, the space and skills of listening to oneself and translating this into better interactions and communication with others.

The communication with oneself is one of the most important and meaningful interactions one can have. But it cannot be separated from one's interactions with one's environment. One cannot determine how one may feel in the presence of a bear, if one has not been exposed to images, descriptions and stories about bears. One cannot know what a good strategy for a relationship is, if one has never been in love with. To explore the inner world successfully, one needs to have interacted with the outside world. What makes it easier is that the rules of communication with the inside world are basically identical with those that apply to the outside world and reducing the barriers between the two is very effective in reducing anxiety.

Interacting with Others

Feeling competent in communicating with others reduces anxiety. This may in part go back to the time where children are totally dependent on their parents for sustenance and to get all their other basic needs met. If primary caregivers, often early on primarily the mother, do not make the baby feel understood, safe and cared for, maybe due to their own insecurities, anxieties or a mood disorder, the anxiety level in the baby is bound to increase, and may stay heightened for years to come into adulthood. However, it may also be that the baby, due in part to a biological predisposition, has less capabilities to make itself understood and convey what t feels, thinks and needs, which then leads to a similar effect. In many cases, there could be heightened anxiety in both, leading to even greater anxiety.

Building a greater sense of competence and efficacy in one's communications with others, helps reverse earlier processes, but it takes some time. The starting point is always the therapeutic session which provides the setting which is most conducive to developing the insight and skills and to activating the autoregulatory processes which lead to greater feelings of competence in communication to get one's needs, values, wishes and aspirations met. The difference to the situation in childhood is that adults have more complex needs and can shape their communication environment, and through it the world around them.

Experiencing the World

To break through the vicious cycle of anxiety, in which emotions like fear and anxiety cause safety thoughts and behaviors, which in turn reinforce feelings of fear, loneliness, sadness, and so forth, it is helpful to focus on identifying what is meaningful and having more of it in life. Communication helps in identifying and finding meaning, either communication with oneself or with others. The exchange of messages is like a learning process in which meaning can be identified, found and accumulated. Through meaningful interactions one accumulates more meaning, more connectedness with oneself and the world and reduces the need for thoughts and behaviors which are triggered by fears, guilt, self-blame and other negative emotions. This also helps against depression and anxiety.

Perceiving more meaning also makes interacting with others and oneself more meaningful. This has a positive effect on one's interaction patterns, how and in which one ways one relates to one's environment and exchanges messages with it.

Values, Needs and Aspirations

Often, individuals suffering from anxiety or burnout have become uncertain about what is really important to them and the fit between these values and interests and their current life situation. Whether in the professional or romantic realms, getting what one needs and values makes happy in the long run, everything else does not. If I value helping people, it is important that I do that to make me happy. At the same time, I might value time spent with friend and spending time by myself. It is important that I can do this in the long run, because otherwise I will not be as happy as I could be.

Meaningful Messages as the Instrument of Change

Communication is the vehicle of change. The instruments are meaningful messages which are generated and received by the people who take part in these interactions. In a therapeutic setting, keeping the mutual flow of information relevant and meaningful brings change in both people who take part in this process. The learning curve for the patient may be steeper in certain respects

because he or she spends less time in this interaction style than a therapist.

Autism and Asperger Syndrome

Introduction

Autism spectrum disorders (ASD) include autism and Asperger syndrome. What they have in common is the difficulties an individual to have interactions with the environment. Individuals with Asperger syndrome can have relationships and be very successful in their jobs.

Communication is the transmission of meaningful messages. Seeing meaning requires being able to understand and see relevance in a message. If an autistic individual is not able to understand a message with regards to a social interaction, he or she cannot see the relevance of the message and cannot consider it meaningful to the own person. This, in turn, may, however, lead to frustration and social withdrawal, rather than learning how to identify and decode messages from other people, and as a consequence oneself.

Especially in lighter forms of autism, such as in Asperger syndrome, there is the potential to understand more if the individual is encouraged and supported in the learning process. At the same time, it is important to help the person with Asperger syndrome to recognize more meaning in oneself and the world around. This also requires learning more about oneself, one's values, interests and aspirations, because these parameters determine what one finds relevant and meaningful.

Autism and Asperger syndrome

Autism is a neurodevelopmental disorder characterized by impaired social interaction, impaired verbal and non-verbal communication, and restricted and repetitive behavior. Parents usually notice signs in the first two years of their child's life. These signs often develop gradually, though some children with autism reach their developmental milestones at a normal pace and then regress. The diagnostic criteria require that symptoms become apparent in early childhood, typically before age three.

Autism is caused by a combination of genetic and environmental factors. Some cases are strongly associated with certain infections during pregnancy including rubella and use of alcohol or cocaine. Autism affects information processing in the brain by altering how nerve cells and their synapses connect and organize. In the DSM V, autism is included within the autism spectrum (ASDs), as is Asperger syndrome, which lacks delays in cognitive development and language, and pervasive developmental disorder, not otherwise specified (commonly abbreviated as PDD-NOS), which was diagnosed when the full set of criteria for autism or Asperger syndrome were not met.

Early speech or behavioral interventions can help children with autism gain self-care, social, and communication skills.

Communication-Focused Therapy (CFT)

Communication-Focused Therapy (CFT) was developed by the author to focus more specifically on the communication process between patient and therapist. The central piece is that the sending and receiving of meaningful messages is at the heart of any change process. CBT, psychodynamic psychotherapy and IPT help because they define a format in which communication processes take place that can bring about change. However, they do not work directly with the communication processes. CFT does so.

The first step is to get a sense for how the patient communicates with himself or herself and the world around, which is necessary to use communication in a therapy session exactly. It is first important to determine how the patient at the moment communicates about own emotions, needs and wishes, and reacts to messages from a therapist and others. This gives clues about thought patterns, beliefs and more which affect how messages from others are interpreted and how own messages are assembled or not sent. What someone sees as meaningful and relevant is largely determined by past experiences with others and with oneself.

The second step is to use this insight in helping the patient to deal with various issues and everyday situations. Often, the two steps run in parallel in an exchange between therapist and patient.

Understanding Autism and Asperger syndrome

Both have in common that there are communication difficulties, both reading other people and reading oneself. People with Asperger syndrome can often work and even excel at it, but interpersonal communication, especially on the emotional level, remains more or less a mystery to them. It is important to convey to a patient the important that emotions can play by working with experiences that seemed encouraging or disturbing and try to identify the own emotions. This also helps identify emotions in others and in oneself.

Meaning

Individuals suffering from anxiety and panic attacks often see less meaning in the things they do. In therapy an important part is to rediscover meaning, and find it in the things that are relevant to the patient. Relevant is anything that is close to his or her values, basic interests, aspirations, wants, wishes and desires.

Communication Training

Communication training means experimenting with communication and then reflecting on it. Communication with another human being means that meaningful messages are exchanged, information that is relevant to be recipient and can be understood by him or her. On the other hand, it also means being able send a message that can be understood by and is relevant to the other. Most species have a combination of hardwired communication programs as well as those that are learned early, but also later, in life. Humans have this combination, too, but with a larger brain area which is freely programmable there is more room to learn communication, and what is probably specific to humans, to learn about communication.

Motivation

One needs to see relevance to oneself and meaning in something to be motivated to engage in it. Especially in patients with autism and ADHD experiencing and feeling that something is relevant to oneself is important. This is not about being selfish, but even being altruistic has to feel good to oneself to be sustainable and have meaning.

One can find relevance and meaning in many things, if the connections between an activity and one's own values and interests is pointed out. In patients with autism, building motivation is no different. One needs to illustrate why learning about communication can help them feel better lives. Unfortunately, often not much time is spent on this absolutely crucial element of therapy.

Observing

To learn about something means having the tools to observe it. Trying to look at cells without a microscope is quite pointless. For an autism patient learning about communication requires some basic structure about what to look for, it requires breaking down communication into its components. This is not only helpful in autism, but also in social anxiety, OCD, and a number of other conditions.

A first step is to identify what one wants from the interaction, another to explore how messages can be sent and received, and what information they can contain. Another unit may deal with how to interpret messages and what they can mean, and what they say about the other person's intentions. A unit on how to respond to messages helps the patient to express own needs and wants in an effective way and imparts a sense of being in control and able to steer the conversation. This can relief the helplessness and pressure from being unable to communicate one's emotions, needs and wants.

Values, Needs and Aspirations

Often, individuals suffering from depression have become uncertain about what is really important to them and the fit between these values and interests and their current life situation. Whether in the professional or romantic realms, getting what one needs and values makes happy in the long run, everything else does not. If I value helping people, it is important that I do that to make me happy. At the same time, I might value time spent with friend and spending time by myself. It is important that I can do this in the long run, because otherwise I will not be as happy as I could be.

Meaningful Messages as the Instrument of Change

While autism or Asperger's syndrome usually remains a diagnosis for life, in the lighter forms a habit of approaching communication with openness and a willingness to learn can make a large difference. In some cases, the need to learn about how to encode and decode messages, sending and receiving, as well as understanding them, can make a person with light autistic features a better communicator than people who never had to become 'experts' at it.

The change resulting form feeling better connected with oneself and with the world raises a patient's confidence and improves his self-image. This in turn can increase the motivation and initiative to communicate even further. In the long-run, experience and practice makes the difference, as long as a patient sees communication as something that can be figured out and finds meaning in it.

In more severe cases of autism, developing a routine in the therapeutic sessions to get the patient more involved in an interaction, providing constructive feedback and supporting him in clearly defined communication steps can achieve significant progress. Rather than using the same plan and the same structures for every patient, the therapeutic work should be highly individualized.

Bipolar Disorder

Introduction

Bipolar disorder is characterized by mood swings in both directions, and although often the down phases tend to be more pronounced and worrying, manic phases can cause significant harm, often financial, to the individual. The less pronounced hypomanic episodes can over the long-run often cause professional, relationship and social problems when individuals work long hours on fleeting projects. The extremes can bring a level of uncertainty, which can lower self-confidence, and have so an effect of how the individual interacts with the world.

Distorted Communication Patterns

Depressed and manic states affect the communication patterns with the world, by which they lead to difficulties and problems with the environment. It can be communication with themselves which makes the depression worse in the form of negative self-talk, self-doubts, and the sense of failure in the face of unrealistic expectations, while in (hypo)manic phases rushing thoughts and extreme expectations can strain interactions with other people, especially if they do not meet the high expectations the person has of itself.

As much as the connection with oneself can be heavily compromised during a depression, it may even be fully lost in a severe manic phase where everything around just becomes an extension of one's own grandiose self, which appears so powerful that its texture with the person's real needs, wants, values and aspirations is lost. All that remains is a shiny balloon, which can pop on everything that is in the way and throw the individual into a deep depression. Especially a manic state is inherently fragile and unsustainable.

Bipolar Disorder

Bipolar disorder, previously known as manic depression, is a mental disorder that causes periods of depression and periods of elevated mood. The elevated mood is significant and is known as mania or hypomania, depending on its severity, or whether symptoms of psychosis are present. During mania, an individual behaves or feels abnormally energetic, happy, or irritable. Individuals often make poorly thought out decisions with little regard to the consequences. The need for sleep is usually reduced during manic phases. During periods of depression, there may be crying, a negative outlook on life, and poor eye contact with others.

The condition is divided into bipolar I disorder if there has been at least one manic episode, with or without depressive episodes, and bipolar II disorder if there has been at least one hypomanic episode (but no manic episodes) and one major depressive episode. In those with less severe symptoms of a prolonged duration, the condition cyclothymic disorder may be diagnosed. If due to drugs or medical problems, it is classified separately.

Treatment commonly includes psychotherapy, as well as medications such as mood stabilizers and antipsychotics. Examples of mood stabilizers that are commonly used include lithium and various anticonvulsants, although atypical (second generation) antipsychotics are used in their own right. Many individuals have financial, social or work-related problems due to the illness. These difficulties occur a quarter to a third of the time on average.

Understanding Bipolar Disorder

Bipolar Disorder means that a patient experiences changes in affective (mood) states which can be disturbing and lead to a sense of instability, which can be threatening to the sense of self and deeply disturbing to the patient. Often, the unpredictability of the mood changes can be as debilitating as the depression or the mania.

In the individual states, suffering is often more conscious in the depressed than in the hypomanic or manic states. When patients come out of the manic states, the sense of regret over huge expenditures, such as through gambling or seemingly random purchases, or other self-harming behavior can be great, and throw the individual into the next depression.

Depressed states have already been outlined above. The problem about the manic states is not primarily the euphoria, but the loss of normal abilities to plan and communicate constructively. In a manic state everything disintegrates, which renders the patient unable to work or, in severe cases, unable to carry out normal everyday tasks.

The reason is that streams of information can no longer be sorted and processed adequately, while cognitive functions, such as focus and memory, are severely impacted.

Affective States and Communication Patterns

Often, there are already maladaptive communication patterns before, that cause the problems in the relationship or interpersonal interactions. However, varying affective states can affect the overall communication behavior and communication patterns of the individual. Often this can self-perpetuate because a maladaptive communication pattern, with its loss of meaningful interactions, can deepen a depression or make a manic individual even more disconnected from his or her environment.

Uncertainty

The sense of uncertainty becomes greater as the affective states become more pronounced. With more effective and meaningful communication these extremes can be cushioned off, because autoregulation through feedback and felt support makes the extremes seem less extreme. Life has its ups and downs and through meaningful interactions with other people a patient can learn how to more effectively deal with these affective variations. This is how better communication can also improve the learning experience from others, which is an important objective in communication-focused therapy.

Communication Deficits

Areas which people often feel anxious about are where there has been an issue with their interpersonal interactions in the past. Early traumata, like a disappearing or abusive parent, stay unresolved. For example, if a parent feels fearful and angry with himself and this is picked up by a child, the latter may decode these messages correctly in that the parent is angry, but since the parent may not be conscious about it, the child does not pick up on the second important half of the message, that the parent has a problem with himself and his issue is unrelated to the child. Of course, one can learn to pick up on the self-blame and frustration of the parent, and therapists should become experts at reading between the lines in this fashion, but it requires experience, reflection and insight into transference and counter-transference phenomena, for example, to use the psychoanalytic terms.

States of depression and mania compromise one's sending and receiving of information. On one hand, there are the negative feelings about oneself and others in depression and the perceived low need for meaningful interactions in manic states which directly interfere with the initiative and motivation to engage in communication with others. On the other hand, the spectrum and openness of interpreting messages and creating new ones is also compromised. The result is that it takes more skills or extra energy to engage with others. Often, seeing more meaning and benefits in communication as a way to fulfill needs but also to see more in life in general can be motivating factors, if the patient sees a personal relevance to it.

Avoidance

Depression can lead to avoidance of others, which has the effect to reduce the mood of the individual even more. Manic states can have a similar effect in the manic state because the (hypo)manic patent gets less from interactions and there is probably a realization, at least subconsciously, that they are lacking in fulfillment, which can intensify the social withdrawal when the manic state wears off. In social situations, not interacting with others deprives the person of an important source of meaning about the world and oneself, while the lack of interactions with others can worsen ruminations in depressive states, which can put additional downward pressure on the patients' self-confidence. Avoidance can thus lead to an increase rather than a decrease in symptoms in the long-run, although the effect is probably larger in the short-run.

Meaning

Individuals suffering from anxiety and panic attacks often see less meaning in the things they do. In therapy an important part is to rediscover meaning and find it in the things that are relevant to the patient. Relevant is anything that is close to his or her values, basic interests, aspirations, wants, wishes and desires.

An important step in therapy thus to make the person aware of how anxiety affects one's thinking. Individuals from anxiety often focus differently from other individuals. There is often a focus on worst outcomes and strong fears which are caused by it. Underlying this are often strong emotions or conflicts which need to be defended against. The danger and uncertainty is quite frequently inside oneself, rather than on the outside. An individual with a fear of flying may be more afraid of not containing oneself and not being able to leave the plain than anything else. Anxiety is the fear of crashing oneself and the feelings of a dreaded uncertainty about oneself and one's emotional states.

Experiencing the World

The world is experienced filtered through the affective extremes. In a depressed episode the world seems like a depressing place, in a manic state like a manically exciting place. As already mentioned, both are not sustainable because of the suffering cause by the affective state in the former and by the consequences of one's actions or inactions in the latter. Over time, the world is experienced as essentially unstable, which then has an effect on how one sees oneself.

To break through the vicious cycle of affective instability, in which depression or the aftermath or a manic state increases the depression and the resentment and negative feelings about oneself, it is helpful to focus on identifying what is meaningful and having more of it in life. The reason is that these parameters remain relatively stable over a person's life-time and being able to experience them also increases the feeling of stability and confidence in oneself.

Communication helps in identifying and finding meaning, either communication with oneself or with others. The exchange of messages is like a learning process in which meaning can be identified, found and accumulated. Through meaningful interactions one accumulates more meaning, more connectedness with oneself and the world and reduces the need for thoughts and behaviors which are triggered by fears, guilt, self-blame and other negative emotions. This also helps against depression and anxiety.

Seeing More

Perceiving more meaning also makes interacting with others and oneself more meaningful. This has a positive effect on one's interaction patterns, how and in which one ways one relates to one's environment and exchanges messages with it. The interactions in the therapeutic setting are important sources to generate more meaning in the world. They also help the patient to create more meaning in self-talk or through helpful thought patterns.

Values, Needs and Aspirations

Often, individuals suffering from anxiety or burnout have become uncertain about what is really important to them and the fit between these values and interests and their current life situation. Whether in the professional or romantic realms, getting what one needs and values makes happy in the long run, everything else does not. If I value helping people, it is important that I do that to make me happy. At the same time, I might value time spent with friend and spending time by myself. It is important that I can do this in the long run, because otherwise I will not be as happy as I could be.

Meaningful Messages as the Instrument of Change

Communication is the vehicle of change. The instruments are meaningful messages which are generated and received by the people who take part in these interactions. In a therapeutic setting, keeping the mutual flow of information relevant and meaningful brings change in both people who take part in this process. The learning curve for the patient may be steeper in certain respects because he or she spends less time in this interaction style than a therapist.

A More Meaningful Reality

Seeing more meaning in reality helps in both, depressed and manic states, to stay closer to a more accurate perception of reality and anchor oneself more firmly in a reality that seems more relevant. Some famous writers and inventors suffered from bipolar disorder, which seemed to influence their descriptions of the ups and downs of life. However, one does not have to suffer from bipolar disorder to experience life intensively. It is more likely that the affective poles make experiences that are unrelated to negative of positive feelings less accessible. The bipolar disorder may only make a non-creative activity more painful and less tolerable than another person might experience it. Seeing the world, and various aspects in it, as more meaningful is what everyone can accomplish.

Borderline Personality Disorder (BPD)

Introduction

For borderline personality disorder various therapeutic approaches have been used with varying success. Since the term is derived from psychoanalytic psychotherapy, a lot of research into BPD has been carried out in that school of psychotherapy. The dynamics of BPD and the intrapsychic structure has largely been described by psychoanalysts and psychodynamic psychotherapists.

CBT has been applied in the form of DBT, which is now widely used in hospitals and outpatient situations in the treatment of BPD. There is significant support for the efficacy of standard dialectical behavior therapy (DBT) for the treatment of suicidal patients who suffer from BPD. However, there is some concern about the long-term effectiveness of CBT and DBT.

Communication at the Core

At the core of any 'talk therapy' is the communication process. It is the mechanism which gets things done and ultimately delivers change towards allowing the patient to have a better life with less symptoms. However, the mentioned therapeutic approaches focus little on the communication process between therapist and patient and inside the patient. This must lower the effectiveness of psychotherapy, particularly when considering that many of the problems patients face because of their condition are interpersonal and interactive in nature. Since the communication with the outside world and the communication a patient is having with himself is tightly linked, the effectiveness of a psychotherapy that deemphasizes the communication aspect must also be limited as regards the psychological state and the self-image of the patient.

Borderline Personality Disorder

Borderline personality disorder (BPD), also known as emotionally unstable personality disorder, is a long-term pattern of abnormal behavior characterized by unstable relationships with other people, unstable sense of self, and unstable emotions. There is often frequent dangerous behavior, a feeling of emptiness, self-harm, and an extreme fear of abandonment. Symptoms may be brought on by seemingly normal events. The behavior typically begins by early adulthood and occurs across a variety of situations. Substance abuse, depression, and eating disorders are commonly associated with BPD.

The Void

The emptiness in BPD is usually quite symptomatic, and self-harm is often a reaction to feel oneself again. Relationships often tend to be unstable, not because an individual with BPD is less able to have one, but because the interaction with another person, or the memory of it, give a feeling of connectedness, which prevents the sensation of an ensuing emptiness, and its loss feels like an existential loss to the person with BPD.

The emptiness and sense of void often seems to be lying over strong emotions. It is a defensive void at the surface, like a blanket that has been thrown over the unruly emotions underneath it. Since there is a disconnect from oneself, the emotions are ill-defined and scary in the sense that they may cause disturbance or damage to the individual. This fear of a core part of oneself keeps the vicious cycle turning, in which fears of fundamental aspects of oneself cause additional fear, distancing from the self, more disconnect, even more fears, more emptiness, more fears, and so on. Communication is the key to break through this pattern.

'Existential Crisis'

The sense of an 'existential crisis' is quite common in BPD, when the individual feels disconnected from oneself and others and feels as if falling into a deep, dark, empty pit. The void is a feeling that communication links, and a sense of nurturing safety, have been severed. It is a loss of faith in communication with oneself and the environment as the tool to satisfy our wants and needs.

Understanding Borderline Personality Disorder

Individuals suffering from BPD experience significant instability because of the importance they attach to connectedness with themselves and others. Often it is not so much the content but that there is an emotional exchange, which makes the person with borderline personality disorder feel safer and more secure.

An approach to BPD is thus to bring in more meaningful content into the interaction and support the patient's reflective and introspective processes. Through questioning and reflecting on apparent conflicts, the patient gets a better sense of him or herself and the interaction with another. This also helps build confidence in oneself and the interaction process with the other.

Patterns of Communication

Individuals with BPD have patterns of communicating with others which often do not seem to work well for them. The patterns are frequently quite rigid in making an interaction about one or a few messages, such as confirmation of the stability of a relationship. This lack of openness probably contributes significantly to the symptoms and relationship difficulties an individual with BPD experiences.

Meaning

Individuals suffering from the type of anxiety ne often sees in BPD often see less meaning in the things they do. In therapy an important part is to rediscover meaning and find it in the things that are relevant to the patient. Relevant is anything that is close to his or her values, basic interests, aspirations, wants, wishes and desires.

Meaning helps to make the world more interesting and counter the sense of emptiness and void. It also is the glue which makes communication interesting and productive.

Dialectic Behavioral Therapy (DBT)

Studies repeatedly find moderate before-and-after effect sizes for global outcomes as well as suicidal and self-injurious behaviors, while the dropout rates are sad to be relatively low. Although DBT is clearly efficacious and increasingly available in practice settings, demand for DBT far exceeds existing resources. The multicomponent nature of DBT (individual therapy, group skills training, between-session telephone coaching, and a therapist consultation team) lends itself to dismantling in clinical settings. Group skills training in DBT is frequently offered alone or, in community mental health settings, with standard case management instead of DBT individual therapy. Other clinicians, often those in private practice, offer DBT individual therapy without any DBT group skills training.

A Manualized Approach

The problem with DBT and most CBT models is that their approach to specific topics or content is highly manualized. This leaves little room for the communication process itself, which interestingly is not manualized, even though it is the component which brings about change. A manualized approach may specify that the patient should be asked about what thought causes sadness, but it is not the topic of the question which causes change. It is that the patient learns how to put together a meaningful message about the sadness she experiences when a certain thought comes up. Once she feels she can do it, the new strategy will be memorized and cause the change in the long-run. If it works for her, adopting the new strategy will be as close to permanent as possible.

No Evidence for the Underlying Mechanisms

The problem is that there is little investigation into what makes DBT or any other kind of psychotherapy work. It is unlikely that it is a particular topic the therapist raises, but what happens in the flow of information between therapist and patient. However, many psychotherapeutic models focus on the former to the exclusion of the latter. The success of psychotherapy is built on Sigmund Freud's original concept of the 'talking cure', which seems to be all but forgotten in many modern approaches. Even interpersonal therapies, such as IPT, focus more on interaction schemata or models rather than the dynamic process of information exchange that underlies any meaningful work in psychotherapy.

Not Individualized

The successes of many psychotherapeutic approaches, including DBT, are moderate at best. This should motivate us to find ways how to improve on existing models. This, however, would require to give up the belief in the exclusive benefit of a specific model, and look at what they have in common. The interaction between human beings, communication, is what they have in common.

Learning to Communicate

Another problem is that any manualized approach which does not focus on the underlying processes directly, will not be individualized enough. It is like giving a student a manual on how to build a specific car rather than teach her engineering, which would allow her to build any car, or other things, she chooses. The fit of the specific manual to be used also depends on the accuracy of the diagnosis, which often tends to be notoriously unreliable, especially if the therapist is still inexperienced. With a manualized approach, however, a poor diagnosis or definition of the problem makes the therapy worthless, unless the therapist focuses on the underlying dynamics, and thus works outside the manual.

The Emotions are not the Problem

The emotions one experiences are not the problem, rather it is how they are communicated on the inside and with the outside world. The disconnection with oneself, which can be found in BPD as well as several other mental health conditions, is the cause of many fears about feeling fragile or unstable, which then trigger very diverse symptoms. Several symptoms in BPD, such as the classical sense of void, the fear of losing oneself or disintegrating, or not being strong enough to withstand emotional stresses, can be explained quite easy with this disconnection. Unfortunately, most schools of psychotherapy treat communication like a black box, which is assumed to do its thing and accepted as a given.

Learning to communicate requires seeing communication and reflecting on it, to be able to use it in novel ways by making it work for oneself. If a patient finds her, or more seldom his, voice, this can go a long way to treating the condition. This is at the core of communication-focused therapy (CFT).

Reconnecting

Better communicating with oneself and others is an important technique towards reconnecting with oneself and the world, which also increases self-confidence, a strengthened sense of self, and increases the sense of effectiveness in getting one's needs and wants met. In the process, many patients also rediscover basic interests, values and old aspirations. All this helps to rebuild a stronger sense of self, which can withstand the emotional gusts or storms, which to a certain extent are part of life.

The process on helping patients to reconnect has already been described above. When working with patients with BPD, it is important to walk through the process with a greater degree of caution so as not to overwhelm the patient whose internal psychic structure already feels fragile. However, a reconnection with one's feelings and thoughts on a meaningful level and developing the skills to reflect on it usually helps fill the void, which is so characteristic of BPD, most of the time. Yet basic parameters, such as values, needs and aspirations, not only bring about more stability and certainty, but they also can have a strong influence on the patient's interactions with other people at the workplace, at home and socially.

Values, Needs and Aspirations

Often, individuals suffering from anxiety or burnout have become uncertain about what is really important to them and the fit between these values and interests and their current life situation. Whether in the professional or romantic realms, getting what one needs and values makes happy in the long run, everything else does not. If I value helping people, it is important that I do that to make me happy. At the same time, I might value time spent with friend and spending time by myself. It is important that I can do this in the long run, because otherwise I will not be as happy as I could be.

Losing the Fear of Communication

Good and meaningful communication requires the ability to send meaningful messages and to receive them. This means openness about oneself and the willingness to engage with the other are important.

Openness

People with BPD often have difficulties with openness because they do not have a good image of themselves. The sense of self does not feel as complete or as whole and this leaves areas of uncertainty or outright bad memories.

Engagement

Engaging with someone else means being open to all kinds of messages, even those which could be potentially hurtful. In BPD messages can have a higher potency to deal a blow to a fragile sense of self, and someone with BPD wants to prevent situations where an existential crisis is felt.

Meaningful Messages as the Instrument of Change

Communication is the vehicle of change; the instruments are meaningful messages which are generated and received by the people who take part in these interactions.

Burnout

Introduction

Burnout is not a diagnosis per se, but it is a quite common condition which often comes with symptoms of anxiety or depression. It is usually a sign that something is out of sync in one's life, that one does not see as much meaning anymore in the things one does and engages in, such as in a job or in a relationship.

Burnout is a condition in which one's activities become deprived of meaning, in connection with a general sense of exhaustion. The loss of meaning seems to increase the negative stress individuals experience, which leads to a greater sense of exhaustion and fatigue. To counter burnout effectively requires increasing the meaning an individual sees in oneself and in the world around.

Burnout

Burnout is primarily associated with the professional world, but there is no reason to see burnout in other areas of life where individuals engage in exhausting activities which become increasingly less meaningful to them. One such example may be in a relationship context, another at school, college or even in a sport or recreational activity. People may even experience burnout on a long vacation. The fundamental components are exhaustion and meaninglessness, when an individual no longer sees the relevance of the activity to oneself, as conducive to one's values, basic interests and aspirations.

Occupational burnout is thought to result from long-term, unresolvable job stress. In 1974, Herbert Freudenberger characterized burnout by a set of symptoms that includes exhaustion resulting from work's excessive demands as well as physical symptoms such as headaches and sleeplessness, "quickness to anger," and closed thinking. He observed that the burned-out worker "looks, acts, and seems depressed".

In order to study burnout, a number of researchers developed more focused conceptualizations of burnout. In one conceptualization, job-related burnout is characterized by emotional exhaustion, depersonalization (treating clients/students and colleagues in a cynical way), and reduced feelings of work-related personal accomplishment. In another conceptualization, burnout is thought to comprise emotional exhaustion, physical fatigue, and cognitive weariness. A third conceptualization holds that burnout consists of exhaustion and disengagement. Burnout is now known to involve the full array of depressive symptoms (e.g., low mood, cognitive alterations, sleep disturbance).

Understanding Burnout

The fear of change often makes it difficult for individuals suffering from burnout to escape the vicious cycle of burnout. As the disconnection from one's work, and by extension form oneself, increases, the recognition of own resources and strengths and the faith in one's competence and sense of efficacy becomes more distant. This increases the feeling of helplessness and hopelessness, which also increases the fear of following the own compass, taking decisions and facing new situations.

It is important to note that a communication disconnect occurs in two directions, towards oneself and other people. Individuals who suffer from burnout often withdraw socially, reduce their interactions in the workplace and at home, and disconnect from themselves. They increasingly miss out on vital information from themselves and from others. The result is not only emotional instability on the inside and emotional flatness towards the outside world and oneself, but also more conflicts with the world and an increased risk of mental and physical health issues.

Fear of Change

Life is constant change. This is important for survival and improvement. However, at the same time there is a need for some level of predictability to be able to make decisions. We need continuity in some respects to be able to weigh off different scenarios in the future. This is why there are laws, rules, science, and other areas of knowledge to help us make decisions. Internally, our values, basic interests and various feelings help us to make decisions that help us align decisions we make in the world with what we need and want. Knowing more about them establishes a greater sense of safety and consistency.

The fear of change is usually lower in people who know more about themselves and about the world. This reduces the fear of change and helps in making better decisions. How to get there is usually through communication. By having a better connection with oneself and the world around the level of meaningful information one has can be increased. But this often requires reducing the fear of communication, the anxiety of openness with oneself and others. Openness is important because communication is inherently a two-way street.

Communication Failures

Burnout often means that communication fails at some level. It may be the communication one has with oneself and with others. Difficulties in identifying one's values, needs and aspirations can lead to a loss of direction, and the more unsure one is about direction the less likely someone is to take on the risk of changing one's job or initiating other changes in one's life.

Unfortunately, someone suffering from burnout may need other people to escape from the breakdown in communication with oneself and others. Communication serves autoregulatory processes, which is common to many biological and psychological processes, but if communication itself becomes the target of anxiousness, which often happens in burnout, it no longer can serve its autoregulatory functions.

Ineffective Communication Patterns

Communication patterns are learned throughout one's life. Many are acquired in childhood and adolescence. Over time, they need more or less significant adjustment and finetuning. Especially if one's life experiences have been unusual, there may need to be adjustment. If one has been beaten or abused as a child, there may be a tendency not to show emotions, not to talk back or overly try to protect oneself when interacting with someone in a role of authority, and possibly of the opposite sex. In adult life, using the same communication patterns can interfere with one's job performance or relationships. One may be more likely to stay in impossible situations, rather than walk away and take the risk of being on one's own or just to say 'No' once in a while. While such a strategy may have afforded some protection early in life, it is now a hindrance, which should be identified in one's interactions with another, such as in psychotherapy setting.

Fear of Own Emotions

Anxiety can lead to avoidance, which in turn can attach even more anxiety to the situations or behaviors which are being avoided. In social situations, not interacting with others deprives the person of continuously updating and honing the skills and confidence of interacting with others. Avoidance can thus lead to an increase rather than a decrease in anxiety in the long-run.

Often psychotherapeutic approaches work with emotions as if they are something that just needs to be sorted and identified. The underlying problem in burnout and many other conditions, however, is that the flow of information from the sources of the emotion is compromised. Emotions do not arise at one point in an organism but are an integration of information that is generated at many places. Awareness of an emotion requires good communication in many places, and while consciousness could never focus on all these packages of information as they are formed in many different places, the interactions in therapy should help a patient become better at perceiving and interpreting the information which she becomes conscious of. This helps to reconnect and is usually quite effective in most stages of burnout treatment.

Fears of Knowing the Self

One can feel oneself without describing it. One feels often oneself if one does things that are meaningful to oneself. Usually this comes with feelings of happiness or joy, while distancing oneself in one's actions and thoughts from oneself leads to uneasiness or negative feelings. One reason people often try to disconnect from or suppress their emotions is to feel themselves less. However, disconnecting from one's values and basic interests leads to bad feelings or a sense of emptiness. Overcoming one's anxiety of communicating with oneself, and also of communicating with others in a meaningful way, usually makes reconnecting much easier and almost automatic.

Meaning

Individuals suffering from borderline often see less genuine meaning in the things they do. In therapy an important part is to rediscover meaning and find it in the things that are relevant to the patient.

Relevant is anything that is close to his or her values, basic interests, aspirations, wants, wishes and desires.

An important step in therapy thus to make the person aware of how continuing in one's present situation affects one's thinking. Individuals in burnout situations often focus differently from other individuals. There is often a focus on worst outcomes and strong fears which are caused by it. Underlying this are often strong emotions or conflicts which need to be defended against. The danger and uncertainty is quite frequently inside oneself, rather than on the outside. An individual with a fear of flying may be more afraid of not containing oneself and not being able to leave the plain than anything else. Anxiety is the fear of crashing oneself and the feelings of a dreaded uncertainty about oneself and one's emotional states.

Experiencing the World

Perceiving more meaning also makes interacting with others and oneself more meaningful. This has a positive effect on one's interaction patterns, how and in which one ways one relates to one's environment and exchanges messages with it.

Meaning

Looking at how someone communicates is an important tool in rediscovering more meaning in one's life and n the world around. Seeing more options and opportunities to engage in often relieves current stress and makes it easier to change a stressful situation in the future.

Relevance

Mindfulness and other approaches can be useful in seeing more in the world. However, it usually starts with finding out more about oneself, because this can lead to seeing more relevance to oneself n the world.

Values, Needs and Aspirations

Often, individuals suffering from anxiety or burnout have become uncertain about what is really important to them and the fit between these values and interests and their current life situation. Whether in the professional or romantic realms, getting what one needs and values makes happy in the long run, everything else does not. If I value helping people, it is important that I do that to make me happy. At the same time, I might value time spent with friend and spending time by myself. It is important that I can do this in the long run, because otherwise I will not be as happy as I could be.

Meaningful Messages as the Instrument of Change

Communication is the vehicle of change. The instruments are meaningful messages which are generated and received by the people who take part in these interactions. In a therapeutic setting, keeping the mutual flow of information relevant and meaningful brings change in both people who take part in this process. The learning curve for the patient may be steeper in certain respects

because he or she spends less time in this interaction style than a therapist.

Real World Change

Once the internal change has happened, the external change is almost automatic. The individual gravitates more openly towards activities which are meaningful and relevant to the individual. This usually does not happen in the short-run, but once the adjustment process has started there is often a sense of feeling liberated. Even staying in a stressful situation in the short-run can be easier to bear if one knows there is light at the end of the tunnel.

Depression

Disconnection

Depression is a general lowering of emotional experiences, while in the lighter forms it may just be a reduction of positive emotional experiences. This emotional disconnect from oneself leads to a less complete of sense of self and lower confidence in oneself and the world. It also affects one's interaction patterns with other people and oneself, which can lead to various problems at the work place, in relationships and other social realms. This in turn can lead to more depressed thoughts and feelings in a vicious cycle.

An important step in fighting depression is becoming inquisitive about how one communicates with oneself and others, looking at the communication patterns one has learned to use, the assumptions on makes about the other's and one's own intentions, wishes and needs, one's values, and many other factors that go into a human interaction where messages are exchanged. All psychotherapies to date work with the human interaction, or to an extent one that is simulated by a computer, as the basic tool in the healing process. However, rather than assuming the process works and shifting the focus to specific content as most of these approaches do, it is worthwhile looking at the communication process itself.

Depression

Depression is a state of low mood and aversion to activity that can affect a person's thoughts, behavior, feelings, and sense of well-being. A depressed mood can be a normal temporary reaction to life events such as loss of a loved one, a job loss, but also 'positive' ones, such as winning in a lottery or having sudden and spectacular success. Such changes in life events can trigger both, episodes of depression and also hypomanic or manic episodes, in which one experiences elation and accelerated thoughts. Physical illnesses can also cause episodes of depression. The common thread in depression is some form of change, which may, however, not be as apparent, or even absent, in some more severe forms of endogenous depression.

Flattening of Emotions

Depression can make sadness and anxiety more prominent and accessible to the individual. However, this is often part of emotions as a whole becoming less accessible. The sadness is also usually not a sadness that resolve itself. Normal emotional processes seem slowed down or inhibited.

Negative Interpretations

Situations and events in the world become more likely to be interpreted as negative, as do one's own actions and thoughts. These interpretations are often relating to the own person, one's sense of self, resources, strengths and weaknesses, and one's values. As one sees oneself as causing negative consequences about oneself and the world, self-blame, feelings of guilt, failure and incompetence emerge. At the same time, the own person, others and the world as a whole have progressively less meaning and relevance to oneself. Especially, this loss of meaning can potentially dangerous situations of self-harm or even suicide. To prevent this requires an insightful and caring use of communication between therapist and patient.

Analyzing Communication Patterns

The first step is to get a sense for how the patient communicates with himself or herself and the world around, which is necessary to use communication in a therapy session exactly. It is first important to determine how the patient communicates in the now about the own emotions, needs and wishes, and reacts to messages from the therapist and others. This gives clues about thought patterns, beliefs and more which affect how messages from others are interpreted and how own messages are assembled or not sent. What someone sees as meaningful and relevant is largely determined by past experiences with others and with oneself.

Insight into Communication

The second step is to use this insight in helping the patient to deal with various issues and everyday situations. Often, the two steps run in parallel in an exchange between therapist and patient.

Insight into communication with others as with oneself are both important because they interact with each other. An individual suffering from depression is less likely to see messages as relevant and meaningful because the own sense of self is reduced. The less patients have a sense of themselves the less likely they are to see a relevance in the information reaching them, whether from inside or outside.

Building the Sense of Self

Depression is a state in which an individual sees less meaning in oneself and in the world around. This is part of a vicious cycle in which autoregulatory processes fail. Seeing less meaning in something means one is less likely to look. In depression the consequence can be further withdrawal from others, but also from oneself.

The most problematic facet in the general loss of meaning in depression is the loss of meaning one perceives in oneself, which, if coupled with aggression, can lead to suicidal thoughts and behaviors. It is thus important to try to steer against this as quickly as possible.

One way of doing this is by rediscovering thoughts, activities or situations which are associated with strong positive emotions, because reactivating these emotions can also increase the connectedness with oneself.

Another way is to rediscover in the communication with the patient what can trigger meaningfulness for the patient. An important way to get there is to make the sense of self more meaningful and relevant to the individual. This can be accomplished by making everything the self is connected to more meaningful.

All these approaches work through communication, and an awareness of the dynamics and processes that occur in the interaction between therapist and patient. Since feelings or emotions are due to the integration of large amounts of information, it is important to check with the patient repeatedly how he feels, especially in depression, where perceiving and identifying feelings is slower and more difficult.

Meaningful Activities

Individuals suffering from depression see less meaning in themselves and in the things they do. In therapy an important part is to rediscover meaning and find it in the things that are relevant to the patient. Relevant is anything that is close to his or her values, basic interests, aspirations, wants, wishes and desires.

Communication is an important part of most activities, either with others or in the constant feedback one has with oneself. Whether it is playing a sport or writing and essay, in everything I do I am constantly checking how I am doing it and how I can improve it, whether this is consciously or subconsciously. Individuals suffering from depression may not give themselves as much positive feedback as would be helpful in maintaining and improving a task. However, as already discussed, n depression there is usually a disconnect with positive as well as with the negative emotions, which makes it more difficult to develop and stay interested in any task. Decisions become more difficult because the necessary information is missing.

Resonance

Messages which resonate with the patient are what brings about the change. These messages can come from the therapist or the patient, they just need to be communicated. If the patient has a particular insight based on some information retrieved from memory or on the perception of a feeling, it is based on information that has been communicated. And the new information resonates if there is something that keeps the focus of attention on it longer than it would on information that does not resonate. In other words, the new information fits into the old information in a special way, it resonates relative to the information contained in the brain.

We are the information we perceive about us. Some information seems so entrenched and reflected in the other information that it comes close to a subjective fact, such as one's values. A depression would have to be so severe that one is disconnected from anything to lose a sense of these basic parameters about oneself, which also provides an angle to work with this information and to build meaning derivatively from the basic parameters.

The interaction between therapist and patient can be meaningful to the patient if what is happening resonates with the values, basic interests or aspirations of the patient. This also means that the therapist, consciously or subconsciously, needs to have a good sense of the patient's values, interests and aspirations, of what is relevant to the patient. This may not only become apparent in what the patient says, but also in what he or she does, and even in the symptoms of the depression and in the situations that attenuate or worsen them.

Communication Exchange

Meaning is built within the exchange in the therapy, the interaction between two human beings, the dynamic which carries the flow of communication and brings it forward. Although depression interferes with the sending and receiving of messages, it does not change the basic process. In a therapeutic session it is important to observe together with the patient what is happening and what the dynamics are and then to use this information to build the interaction patterns which allow to reflect on the patient's basic parameters and support the patient in interacting better with herself and the world with a view to achieving more happiness. While reflecting directly on unhelpful interaction, thought and behavioral pattern which maintain the depression can be helpful, a long-term oriented strategy is often to replace the depression over time with new perspectives, new focus and new ways of reflecting on one's thinking and feelings.

In the long run, perceived meaning can be integrated into the concept a patient has of himself, since individuals derive meaning from interacting with themselves and with other people around them. This also increases the significance and meaningfulness a patient attaches to himself, which in clinical experience helps against depression in two ways. First, it increases the motivation and initiative to engage in activities which has an anti-depression effect. Secondly, a more positive sense of self directly lowers a feeling of being depressed, partly by reducing the negative thought loops, which lowers depression through a learning effect.

Basic Parameters (Values, Needs and Aspirations)

Often, individuals suffering from depression have become uncertain about what is really important to them and the fit between these values and interests and their current life situation. Whether in the professional or romantic realms, getting what one needs and values makes happy in the long run, everything else does not. If I value helping people, it is important that I do that to make me happy. At the same time, I might value time spent with friend and spending time by myself. It is important that I can do this in the long run, because otherwise I will not be as happy as I could be.

Meaningful Messages as the Instrument of Change

Communication is the vehicle of change; the instruments are meaningful messages which are generated and received by the people who take part in these interactions. In depression, the desired change is for a broader emotional experience, seeing more relevance in oneself, one's thoughts and emotions, and in the world as a whole.

Broader Experience

If there is more meaning in oneself and the world, it is easier to focus on aspects of oneself and of the world. This expands one's experience of oneself and of the world around. Seeing more relevance and more sources of novelty and change in the world, increases one's experience of the world and makes this experience richer.

Eating Disorders

Introduction

The act of eating has some attributes in common with communication. Like communication, eating is necessary for survival, and in fact in infants, communication is a prerequisite to being fed when one is hungry. Later in life, communication still plays an important role in maintaining sustenance. One the other hand, eating makes life and communication possible. Thus, there is an interdependence between eating and communication.

Eating Disorders

An eating disorder is a mental disorder defined by abnormal eating habits that negatively affect a person's physical or mental health. They include binge eating disorder where people eat a large amount in a short period of time, anorexia nervosa where people eat very little and thus have a low body weight, bulimia nervosa where people eat a lot and then try to rid themselves of the food, pica where people eat non-food items, rumination disorder where people regurgitate food, avoidant/restrictive food intake disorder where people have a lack of interest in food, and a group of other specified feeding or eating disorders. Anxiety disorders, depression, and substance abuse are common among people with eating disorders.

Each eating disorder seems to come with its own distinct communication patterns, both internally and externally. How patients suffering from anorexia or bulimia communicate and view themselves and communicate with others differs enormously. In anorexia, there is often a difference in how a patient sees her own body from how others see it, while this is not necessarily the case in bulimia. In bulimia, however, there are often patterns in interactions and relationships with others, which may be mostly absent in anorexia. The eating problem and any communication problems, which also includes how information and meaning is processes, seem to go hand in hand.

Causes

Both biological and environmental factors appear to play a role. Cultural idealization of thinness is believed to contribute. Eating disorders affect about 12 percent of dancers. Those who have experienced sexual abuse are also more likely to develop eating disorders.

Treatment

Treatment typically involves counselling, a proper diet, a normal amount of exercise, and the reduction of efforts to eliminate food. Hospitalization is occasionally needed. Medications may be used to help with some of the associated symptoms.

Communication as Therapy

Working in a meaningful communication setting is what can bring about significant changes in the treatment of eating disorders. It consists of three parts, getting patients interested and to engage in communication, to identify what is important and of value to the patient, and to identify and change communication patterns which seem related to the specific eating disorder. Often these steps runs in parallel, but it is important to see them as important components and that all three are required to effect lasting change.

Eating Disorders

An eating disorder is a mental disorder defined by abnormal eating habits that negatively affect a person's physical or mental health. They include binge eating disorder where people eat a large amount in a short period of time, anorexia nervosa where people eat very little and thus have a low body weight, bulimia nervosa where people eat a lot and then try to rid themselves of the food, pica where people eat non-food items, rumination disorder where people regurgitate food, avoidant/restrictive food intake disorder where people have a lack of interest in food, and a group of other specified feeding or eating disorders. Anxiety disorders, depression, and substance abuse are common among people with eating disorders. These disorders do not include obesity.

The cause of eating disorders is not clear. Both biological and environmental factors appear to play a role. Cultural idealization of thinness is believed to contribute. Eating disorders affect about 12 percent of dancers. Those who have experienced sexual abuse are also more likely to develop eating disorders. Some disorders such as pica and rumination disorder occur more often in people with intellectual disabilities. Only one eating disorder can be diagnosed at a given time.

Treatment can be effective for many eating disorders. This typically involves counselling, a proper diet, a normal amount of exercise, and the reduction of efforts to eliminate food. Hospitalization is occasionally needed. Medications may be used to help with some of the associated symptoms. At five years about 70% of people with anorexia and 50% of people with bulimia recover. Recovery from binge eating disorder is less clear and estimated at 20% to 60%. Both anorexia and bulimia increase the risk of death.

In the developed world binge eating disorder affects about 1.6% of women and 0.8% of men in a given year. Anorexia affects about 0.4% and bulimia affects about 1.3% of young women in a given year. Up to 4% of women have anorexia, 2% have bulimia, and 2% have binge eating disorder at some point in time.   Anorexia and bulimia occur nearly ten times more often in females than males. Typically, they begin in late childhood or early adulthood. Rates of other eating disorders are not clear. Rates of eating disorders appear to be lower in less developed countries.

Learning to Communicate

Better communicating with oneself and others goes a long way to feel disconnected from oneself and others. However, it is this disconnection which causes several symptoms in BPD, such as the classical sense of void, the fear of losing oneself or disintegrating, or not being strong enough to withstand the emotional storms one feels are raging inside oneself. Unfortunately, most schools of psychotherapy treat communication like a black box, which is assumed to do its thing and accepted as a given.

Learning to communicate requires seeing communication and reflecting on it, to be able to use it in novel ways by making it work for oneself. If a patient finds her, or more seldom his, voice, this can go a long way in treating the condition.

Eating Disorders

Borderline personality disorder (BPD), also known as emotionally unstable personality disorder, is a long-term pattern of abnormal behavior characterized by unstable relationships with other people, unstable sense of self, and unstable emotions. There is often frequent dangerous behavior, a feeling of emptiness, self-harm, and an extreme fear of abandonment. Symptoms may be brought on by seemingly normal events. The behavior typically begins by early adulthood and occurs across a variety of situations. Substance abuse, depression, and eating disorders are commonly associated with BPD.

The Void

The emptiness in BPD is usually quite symptomatic, and self-harm is often a reaction to feel oneself again. Relationships often tend to be unstable, not because an individual with BPD is less able to have one, but because the interaction with another person, or the memory of it, give a feeling of connectedness, which prevents the sensation of an ensuing emptiness, and its loss feels like an existential loss to the person with BPD.

The emptiness and sense of void often seems to be lying over strong emotions. It is a defensive void at the surface, like a blanket that has been thrown over the unruly emotions underneath it. Since there is a disconnect from oneself, the emotions are ill-defined and scary in the sense that they may cause disturbance or damage to the individual. This fear of a core part of oneself keeps the vicious cycle turning, in which fears of fundamental aspects of oneself cause additional fear, distancing from the self, more disconnect, even more fears, more emptiness, more fears, and so on. Communication is the key to break through this pattern.

Patterns of Communication

Individuals with BPD have patterns of communicating with others which often do not seem to work well for them. The patterns are frequently quite rigid in making an interaction about one or a few messages, such as confirmation of the stability of a relationship. This lack of openness probably contributes significantly to the symptoms and relationship difficulties an individual with BPD experiences.

Understanding Eating Disorders

Individuals suffering from BPD experience significant instability because of the importance they attach to connectedness with themselves and others. Often it is not so much the content but that there is an emotional exchange, which makes the person with borderline personality disorder feel safer and more secure.

An approach to BPD is thus to bring in more meaningful content into the interaction and support the patient's reflective and introspective processes. Through questioning and reflecting on apparent conflicts, the patient gets a better sense of him or herself and the interaction with another. This also helps build confidence in oneself and the interaction process with the other.

'Existential Crisis'

The sense of an 'existential crisis' is quite common in BPD, when the individual feels disconnected from oneself and others and feels as if falling into a deep, dark, empty pit. The void is a feeling that communication links, and a sense of nurturing safety, have been severed. It is a loss of faith in communication with oneself and the environment as the tool to satisfy our wants and needs.

Meaning

Individuals suffering from the type of anxiety ne often sees in BPD often see less meaning in the things they do. In therapy an important part is to rediscover meaning and find it in the things that are relevant to the patient. Relevant is anything that is close to his or her values, basic interests, aspirations, wants, wishes and desires.

Meaning helps to make the world more interesting and counter the sense of emptiness and void. It also is the glue which makes communication interesting and productive.

Values, Needs and Aspirations

Often, individuals suffering from anxiety or burnout have become uncertain about what is really important to them and the fit between these values and interests and their current life situation. Whether in the professional or romantic realms, getting what one needs and values makes happy in the long run, everything else does not. If I value helping people, it is important that I do that to make me happy. At the same time, I might value time spent with friend and spending time by myself. It is important that I can do this in the long run, because otherwise I will not be as happy as I could be.

Losing the Fear of Communication

Good and meaningful communication requires the ability to send meaningful messages and to receive them. This means openness about oneself and the willingness to engage with the other are important.

Openness

People with BPD often have difficulties with openness because they do not have a good image of themselves. The sense of self does not feel as complete or as whole and this leaves areas of uncertainty or outright bad memories.

Engagement

Engaging with someone else means being open to all kinds of messages, even those which could be potentially hurtful. In BPD messages can have a higher potency to deal a blow to a fragile sense of self, and someone with BPD wants to prevent situations where an existential crisis is felt.

Meaningful Messages as the Instrument of Change

Communication is the vehicle of change; the instruments are meaningful messages which are generated and received by the people who take part in these interactions.

Narcissism

Introduction

Narcissism is related to how an individual communicates with oneself. At the core of the condition, which can significantly interfere with one's life, is a loss of connection with oneself, one's values, basic interests, needs, wants and aspirations, the parameters which make oneself feel as oneself. The result is that there is a large unknown which can lead to fears about oneself and lower self-confidence.

Communication on the Inside

For various reasons the sense of self can seem incomplete, fractured or deficient. Often traumatic interpersonal experiences, and frequently prolonged low-level ones, can make it difficult to conceive of a self that is an effective support in the background. Rather, it becomes an issue because the usual communication and interaction processes, which are under normal circumstances what brings out the sense of a self, are used in self-defense rather as mutually constructive processes.

Communication between the Inside and Outside Worlds

The outside world becomes more important to someone suffering from narcissism because, feeling less about oneself, the individual tries to find part of the self and a connection with it in others. However, the weak sense of self on the inside makes holding apart the inside and outside worlds more difficult, not to the extent in psychosis or in Borderline disorder, but to keep them apart requires some activity, which is in an overcompensation in the outside world. Since the inside world remains partly unknown, the narcissist relies more on the outside than the inside world.

Communication as Therapy

Communication is an important tool to resolve this by helping the individual have a better contact with himself or herself again. Through the therapeutic process the individual can complete some of the work to build a stable sense of self by inquiring in a safe environment into the own needs, wants, values and aspirations. This happens partly by reflecting on past life experiences and partly by connecting better with one's own emotions. The objective should be a more meaningful flow of information on the inside, as well as between the inside and the outside world.

Narcissism

Narcissism is the pursuit of gratification from vanity or egotistic admiration of one's own attributes. The term originated from Greek mythology, where the young Narcissus fell in love with his own image reflected in a pool of water. Narcissism is a concept in psychoanalytic theory, which was popularly introduced in Sigmund Freud's essay On Narcissism (1914). The American Psychiatric Association has listed the classification narcissistic personality disorder in its Diagnostic and Statistical Manual of Mental Disorders (DSM) since 1968, drawing on the historical concept of megalomania.

Avoiding being Really Seen

Narcissism is not the same as egocentrism. Rather than wanting to be at the center of the world, narcissists are afraid that they could be seen for who they really are. A narcissist's self-image is either diffuse or deficient, at least much of the time. Often, this is compensated for by portraying images of greatness and success, which masks the fear of connecting with oneself and conceals one's sense of self to others.

Understanding Narcissism

Narcissism is linked to one's communication patterns, because it tries to conceal and project images of oneself at the same time. Since this is difficult to accomplish in the long-run, problems and symptoms ensue.   Often, relationships become fragile and the performance in the work-place, though frequently high, suffers because it becomes difficult to maintain thoughts and actions which do not feel authentic and true to oneself.

To solve this, it is important to raise the patient's confidence and faith in the effectiveness of a more complete communication with himself or herself. Openness and transparency, which are scary to the narcissist, actually represent part of the solution. This require reducing fears of a fuller communication with oneself and others.

Faith in Communication

The faith in one's own ability of an effective communication with others, through which own wants and needs can be met often needs to be rebuilt in someone suffering from narcissism.

Meaning

Meaning only exists partially in the world to the narcissist because of the disconnect from oneself. Reconnecting with values, interests and aspirations is an important step to increase meaning. At the same time, emotional difficulties from the past may need to be resolved to make an emotional reconnection possible.

An important step in therapy thus to make the person aware of how the fear of connecting with oneself affects one's thinking. Individuals from anxiety often focus differently from other individuals. There is often a focus on worst outcomes and strong fears which are caused by it. Underlying this are often strong emotions or conflicts which need to be defended against. The danger and uncertainty is quite frequently inside oneself, rather than on the outside. An individual with a fear of flying may be more afraid of not containing oneself and not being able to leave the plain than anything else. Anxiety is the fear of crashing oneself and the feelings of a dreaded uncertainty about oneself and one's emotional states.

Experiencing the World

To break through the vicious cycle of anxiety, in which emotions like fear and anxiety cause safety thoughts and behaviors, which in turn reinforce feelings of fear, loneliness, sadness, and so forth, it is helpful to focus on identifying what is meaningful and having more of it in life. Communication helps in identifying and finding meaning, either communication with oneself or with others. The exchange of messages is like a learning process in which meaning can be identified, found and accumulated. Through meaningful interactions one accumulates more meaning, more connectedness with oneself and the world and reduces the need for thoughts and behaviors which are triggered by fears, guilt, self-blame and other negative emotions. This also helps against depression and anxiety.

Perceiving more meaning also makes interacting with others and oneself more meaningful. This has a positive effect on one's interaction patterns, how and in which one ways one relates to one's environment and exchanges messages with it.

Values, Needs and Aspirations

Often, individuals suffering from anxiety or burnout have become uncertain about what is really important to them and the fit between these values and interests and their current life situation. Whether in the professional or romantic realms, getting what one needs and values makes happy in the long run, everything else does not. If I value helping people, it is important that I do that to make me happy. At the same time, I might value time spent with friend and spending time by myself. It is important that I can do this in the long run, because otherwise I will not be as happy as I could be.

Meaningful Messages as the Instrument of Change

Communication is the vehicle of change. The instruments are meaningful messages which are generated and received by the people who take part in these interactions. In a therapeutic setting, keeping the mutual flow of information relevant and meaningful brings change in both people who take part in this process. The learning curve for the patient may be steeper in certain respects because he or she spends less time in this interaction style than a therapist.

Obsessive-Compulsive Disorder (OCD)

Introduction

Cognitive Behavioral Therapy (CBT), interpersonal psychotherapy and psychodynamic psychotherapy are often used to treat OCD. However, they rely on explanations of why they work, such as learning, internal conflicts or relationship, which seem to neglect the fundamental process which is common to all psychotherapy, communication.

Psychodynamic Psychotherapy and CBT

Both therapeutic approaches have shown effectiveness in the treatment of anxiety and panic attacks. Both have theories about why they help. The former sees learning processes about certain thought processes as central, the latter psychodynamic processes that bring about a change. However, they both neglect the communication process and changes in how people communicate as what ultimately helps. The difference to interpersonal psychotherapy is that the latter focuses more on the interpersonal setting and situation than the communication processes.

Understanding OCD

OCD and anxiety are related to how people communicate with themselves and with others. They often occur when a relationship breaks apart or some other interpersonal change or issue causes. The result is often communicative patterns that are maladaptive to the individual. These changes in communication patterns are what causes then the problems to the individuals.

Often, there are already maladaptive communication patterns before, that cause the problems in the relationship or interpersonal interactions. These patterns can be analyzed and changed. Another important element is that communication can also take place on the inside of the individual.

Meaning

Individuals suffering from anxiety and OCD often see less meaning in the things they do. In therapy an important part is to rediscover meaning and find it in the things that are relevant to the patient. Relevant is anything that is close to his or her values, basic interests, aspirations, wants, wishes and desires. The more one sees that particular thoughts or actions are relevant to one's own life, the easier it is to engage in them and the more likely are they to become a meaningful part of one's life and oneself.

Intrusive thoughts in OCD appear relevant to one's life, and this is what makes OCD harder to treat than many other conditions. An important step in therapy thus is to make the person aware of how

OCD affects one's thinking. The intrusive thought itself is not the problem, as they occur in most people. Individuals with OCD process these thoughts differently. They experience emotions and attach a relevance to them which seems to make them meaningful and relevant to the individual. Especially the emotions that are triggered cause yet other emotions, such as fear leading to anger or a need for security, which maintain the thoughts and rituals in OCD.

To break through the vicious cycle of OCD, in which emotions like fear and anxiety cause safety thoughts and behaviors, which in turn reinforce feelings of fear, loneliness, sadness, and so forth, it is helpful to focus on identifying what is meaningful and having more of it in life. Communication helps in identifying and finding meaning, either communication with oneself or with others. The exchange of messages is like a learning process in which meaning can be identified, found and accumulated. Through meaningful interactions one accumulates more meaning, more connectedness with oneself and the world and reduces the need for thoughts and behaviors which are triggered by fears, guilt, self-blame and other negative emotions. This also helps against depression and anxiety.

Perceiving more meaning also makes interacting with others and oneself more meaningful. This has a positive effect on one's interaction patterns, how and in which one ways one relates to one's environment and exchanges messages with it.

Values, Needs and Aspirations

Often, individuals suffering from anxiety or burnout have become uncertain about what is really important to them and the fit between these values and interests and their current life situation. Whether in the professional or romantic realms, getting what one needs and values makes happy in the long run, everything else does not. If I value helping people, it is important that I do that to make me happy. At the same time, I might value time spent with friend and spending time by myself. It is important that I can do this in the long run, because otherwise I will not be as happy as I could be.

Getting an eye for what is meaningful helps in identifying own values, needs and aspirations. In this sense, meaningful communication is a learning process in which a sense for relevance can be nurtured. Changes in one's life begin with the ability to select and filter information, such as that contained in perceptions and thoughts, to make it useful. In OCD, this filter does not work efficiently. However, through interactions with the outside world, the filter with regards to the inner world can be reestablished and maintained.

Meaningful Messages as the Instrument of Change

Communication is the vehicle of change. The instruments are meaningful messages which are generated and received by the people who take part in these interactions. In a therapeutic setting, keeping the mutual flow of information relevant and meaningful brings change in both people who take part in this process. The learning curve for the patient may be steeper in certain respects because he or she spends less time in this interaction style than a therapist.

Paranoia

Introduction

Paranoia is a central symptom of psychosis. But it is more than just a symptom, it is a way of perceiving, thinking and communicating which deserves to be looked at separately. It can be a feature of depression and various other conditions which are not psychotic illnesses per se.

A central feature of paranoia is that the patent becomes a reference point for various events in the world. An individual suffering from paranoia interprets events in the world as linked to the own person and projects motives into other people which do not exist. Some paranoid thoughts may be so close to reality that it is different to distinguish what is paranoid and what is not. For example, someone who goes through a stressful relationship breakup or works at a chaotic work place may see intentions in others which could well exist.

As a Psychotic Symptom

Psychosis can be very debilitating to the individual. It is a condition in which the separation between the outside and the inside worlds becomes tenuous. Thoughts may be perceived as real outside events, such as in the form of voices, and outside events seems to have direct effects on the internal worlds.

Conviction

The distinguishing characteristic of a paranoid thought is often the totality in conviction which cannot be reached with reasoning. In the real world, things are rarely as unassailable as a paranoid thought, which is not scrutinized and reflected upon. It just seems to be there.

Communication Therapy

In the therapeutic setting the therapist and patient can experiment with different perspectives and explanations for the patient's perspective. Training this with the patient can help the patient to protect at least against new paranoid thoughts. It can also help to soften up the old ones to a degree. However, what usually helps most is to help the patient reconnect with oneself. Especially access to the emotions that may be associated with and maintain the paranoid thought can break up the paranoid thought. This usually works better if the paranoid thought is not symptoms of a severe depression, which should be treated first. If there is an underlying condition like a depression or schizophrenia, the paranoia disappears once the condition has been treated successfully.

The Boundary between Inside and Outside

What distinguishes the outside from the inside world is how individuals perceive and process information flows. Thus, by addressing how one communicates with oneself and the environment, it is possible to do something effectively against the symptoms of psychosis. By learning how to use communication more correctly, the patent can learn to distinguish better between the world on the inside and the world on the outside.

Paranoia

Paranoia is a central symptom of psychosis. Paranoia is an instinct or thought process believed to be heavily influenced by anxiety or fear, often to the point of delusion and irrationality. Paranoid thinking typically includes persecutory, or beliefs of conspiracy concerning a perceived threat towards oneself. Paranoia is distinct from phobias, which also involve irrational fear, but usually no blame. Making false accusations and the general distrust of others also frequently accompany paranoia. For example, an incident most people would view as an accident or coincidence, a paranoid person might believe was intentional.

Paranoid cognition is a manifestation of an intra-psychic conflict/disturbance. The biases of blaming others for one's problems serve to alleviate the distress produced by the feeling of being humiliated, and helps to repudiate the belief that the self is to blame for such incompetence. This intra-psychic perspective emphasize that the cause of paranoid cognitions are inside the head of the people (social perceiver), and dismiss the fact that paranoid cognition may be related with the social context in which such cognitions are embedded. This point is extremely relevant because when origins of distrust and suspicion (two components of paranoid cognition) are studied many researchers have accentuated the importance of social interaction, particularly when social interaction has gone awry. Even more, a model of trust development pointed out that trust increase or decrease as a function of the cumulative history of interaction between two or more persons.

Psychosis

Psychosis is an abnormal condition of the mind that involves a loss of contact with reality. There may be acoustic or visual hallucinations and paranoid beliefs. People experiencing psychosis may exhibit personality changes and thought disorder. Depending on its severity, this may be accompanied by unusual or bizarre behavior, as well as difficulty with social interaction and impairment in carrying out daily life activities. However, even the bizarre behavior makes sense if the therapist tries to develop an understanding for how the patient takes in information, identifies the source of it and processes it. The bizarre behaviors or thoughts should be seen as reactions to how the patient sees and perceives the world in the specific framework of the individual communication experience.

Communication Patterns

In a diagnostic sense, a new-onset episode of psychosis is not considered a symptom of a psychiatric disorder until other relevant and known causes of psychosis are properly excluded. However, it is important to understand that, no matter what the course, if the perception, thought and reaction patterns are the same, chances are high that information is received and processed in a similar way, that is the communication framework through which the patent communicates with herself and the outside world are similar or even the same.

Understanding Paranoia

Paranoia is essentially a problem in the communication system. If there are certain emotions, especially conflicting ones, and there is a problem in identifying accurately the source of information, an emotion of anger or sadness can lead to someone being followed by a secret agent or a member of a conspiracy. Often, if there is a paranoia about being pursued, the pursuer is unspecific, a person without an identity. This may be sometimes different in severe depressions where someone feels pursued by a specific person. However, more common, is the conviction of being pursued by an amorphous mass or people without a specific identity. The reason can be found in the emotions behind the paranoid thought, which are amorphous themselves, except for the emotional quality they possess.

Experiencing the World

To break through the vicious cycle of anxiety, in which emotions like fear and anxiety cause safety thoughts and behaviors, which in turn reinforce feelings of fear, loneliness, sadness, and so forth, it is helpful to focus on identifying what is meaningful and having more of it in life. Communication helps in identifying and finding meaning, either communication with oneself or with others. The exchange of messages is like a learning process in which meaning can be identified, found and accumulated. Through meaningful interactions one accumulates more meaning, more connectedness with oneself and the world and reduces the need for thoughts and behaviors which are triggered by fears, guilt, self-blame and other negative emotions. This also helps against depression and anxiety.

Perceiving more meaning also makes interacting with others and oneself more meaningful. This has a positive effect on one's interaction patterns, how and in which one ways one relates to one's environment and exchanges messages with it.

Values, Needs and Aspirations

Often, individuals suffering from anxiety or burnout have become uncertain about what is really important to them and the fit between these values and interests and their current life situation. Whether in the professional or romantic realms, getting what one needs and values makes happy in the long run, everything else does not. If I value helping people, it is important that I do that to make me happy. At the same time, I might value time spent with friend and spending time by myself. It is important that I can do this in the long run, because otherwise I will not be as happy as I could be.

Diversity of Experiences

The creation of meaning in the therapeutic can help the patient see more relevance in the 'real' world, which, together with a better adapted processing of information, can protect against paranoid thoughts and read meaning in events more accurately. Thus, the meaningful and relevant interactions the patient engages in can help to lower paranoid thoughts, but at the same time also direct the focus towards things and activities which are really of value to the patient.

Connecting with others and connecting with oneself can go hand in hand. In both one learns about communication, reflecting on thoughts and how the mind works. This provides the tools and skills to be more effective in one's interactions with the environment. However, it also helps to build better suited and more stable structure in oneself, which help see and process the perceptions of the world better and help the individual to have a better understanding of the world. Paranoia can only exist where the understanding of something is deficient, unless one is such a severe psychotic state that the boundaries between inside and outside world, between cognitive knowledge, emotions, and information received from the outside world, is lost.

Meaningful Messages as the Instrument of Change

Communication is the vehicle of change. The instruments are meaningful messages which are generated and received by the people who take part in these interactions. In a therapeutic setting, keeping the mutual flow of information relevant and meaningful brings change in both people who take part in this process. The learning curve for the patient may be steeper in certain respects because he or she spends less time in this interaction style than a therapist.

Integration

The objective of communication-focused therapy is to help the patient reintegrate free floating and dissociated emotions, unreflected and untested thoughts and perceptions about oneself and the world into a stable and helpful sense of self. As described, paranoid thoughts usually weaken in a meaningful communication between therapist and patient. The important part in the process is finding what is behind the paranoid thoughts, which usually leads to their collapse. However, since there is a learned component to paranoid thought, it may take the patient some time to unlearn them. In any case, once an emotion behind the paranoid thoughts has been understood by another and the patient, it usually resolves itself.

If there are other psychiatric conditions underlying the paranoid thoughts and maintaining their dynamic, treating them is also an important component in the treatment of the paranoid thoughts.

Psychosis

Introduction

Psychosis means losing touch with reality in one's perception of what is real. It is thus a failure in meaningful communication. Medication is often the first-line treatment, and many psychotherapy schools are reluctant to work with people suffering from psychotic symptoms. However, underlying most psychotherapies is the belief in the effectiveness of interpersonal communication, the 'talk therapy'. Since in psychosis there are patterns of communication with oneself and others that are causing symptoms and are not helpful to the individual, using therapy to change them can be very helpful in the treatment and management of psychosis.

Learning through Communication

Learning to identify better the sources of information, inside one's own body and in the outside world, can help to attach the correct meaning to a sensation or a voice one hears. This should be trained in the communication space of a psychotherapeutic setting.

Resources

Patients suffering from psychosis often lose a sense of their own resources because the self becomes fleeting and less accessible. In the therapeutic interaction, through the communication process a more stable distinction between the inside and outside worlds can be established, which strengthens the sense of self, and thus makes the own resources more accessible.

Psychosis

Psychosis is an abnormal condition of the mind that involves a loss of contact with reality. People experiencing psychosis may exhibit personality changes and thought disorder. Depending on its severity, this may be accompanied by unusual or bizarre behavior, as well as difficulty with social interaction and impairment in carrying out daily life activities. Generally, psychosis involves noticeable deficits in normal behavior (negative signs) and more commonly to diverse types of hallucinations or delusional beliefs, particularly with regard to the relation between self and others as in grandiosity and pronoia or paranoia. Unfortunately, psychosis as a diagnostic term is often used after other reasons have been excluded.

Sources of Information

As the information can no longer be correctly attributed to an outside or an inside source, the individual experiences own thoughts coming from outside in the form of voices or people on the outside as part of internal mental processes and might experience this as people having influence on the own thoughts.

A Diversity of Symptoms

As can be imagined from the underlying mechanism, a host of symptoms is possible. Psychosis is a descriptive term for the hallucinations, delusions and impaired insight that may occur as part of a psychiatric disorder. All these symptoms go back to a misinterpretation of the source of information or a misinterpretation of the meaning of the message. Working with individuals with psychosis can be very satisfying professionally, because once a patient learns to identify sources more correctly by making a habit of testing convictions and becomes more open to information from the inside and the outside, the reduction in symptoms is in clinical experience almost automatic. This does not mean one can waive the need for medication, but it often helps to reduce the dose and give the patient back a greater sense of self-esteem, self-efficacy and satisfaction.

Understanding Psychosis

In psychosis the internal and external worlds cannot be distinguished as accurately anymore. They seem to blend into each other. This can cause various symptoms that are then summarized as 'psychotic'. However, each symptom should make sense in the context of the patient's communication patterns as well as the life experiences and emotions the patient faces, which influence the content of the psychosis. Having an understanding for what is happening, is important because it also helps make the patient feel more secure, which is one of the first things the psychosis takes away, often already in the prodromal phase. Lowering fear and anxiety are important steps in managing and treating psychosis.

Besides the inability to distinguish internal from external sources, psychosis also leads to misinterpretation of messages, which is not only a result of misjudging their sources. The decoding and understanding of messages suffers, which makes them unreadable. This raises the uncertainty about oneself and others because less relevant information reaches the patient. Consequently, fears and anxieties increase.

Meaningful Communication

When an individual suffers from psychosis, a first important step is to help the patient see meaning in the communication process, particularly a relevance to own needs and interests. This helps to build and maintain the motivation which is necessary for a communication oriented therapeutic process. To accomplish this, it is important to give the patient the space needed so that he can feel safe and does not feel judged. If the patient can talk, everything he says should be used to try to understand what he is trying to communicate. If the patient does not talk, sometimes it helps to talk about the situation. Just by being open and reflecting on how one sees and feels about the situation rather than questioning or talking directly about the patient, a sense of trust and shared experience can be built. Often, even if a patient does not talk, just being there and displaying openness and transparency can reduce fears and lower the threshold for the patent to engage at his own pace in an interaction with the therapist. All this may take time, but in the long-run this investment is usually worth it.

Learning about Communication

The first step is to learn about communication, to see how it works, what its constituents are and the purposes it can serve. Often it helps to go through examples that may be of special relevance to the patient. Analyzing them and looking at different options and different outcomes help to illustrate to the patient the importance of the process.

Observing Communication

Splitting up communication and being able to identify its components helps to observe the process and the variations, large and small, in it. Observing is not only a learning experience, but also helps to develop interest for it and see where the process can be influenced.

Observing can already occur in the first session, even before a first verbal contact has been made. It is important for a therapist, who is accustomed to observing people, to appreciate that the patient is also observing the therapist and draws his own conclusions. Usually when strangers meet, the first thing they engage in is observing each other and building theories about the other person. Here the therapist needs to remember that psychosis does not cause hostility or fear per se, but that the patient may not decode the information from the therapist or about himself the same way as the therapist. This means that the therapist should not only be open to the unfolding process but make as little assumptions about the patient's inner world and way of thinking as possible. If the patient speaks, listening attentively and carefully asking non-confrontational and non-intrusive questions in most cases provides the information one needs.

The important next step is to observe together and to share the observations. Over time, this builds a strong therapeutic alliance and a firm basis for trust between the therapist and the patient. From a communication perspective, it shines the spotlight on the dynamic in which new patterns and strategies can be developed for the outside world.

Experimenting

Experimenting with communication in its different flavors can give the patient a greater sense of effectiveness with respect to the environment as well as oneself. It gives patients a greater sense of being in control, which is helpful because patients with psychosis often experience helpless and hopelessness, which can also cause some of the sudden emotional outbursts seen in severe cases of psychosis, such as schizophrenia.

Reflecting

The newly gained knowledge and skills around communication needs to be processed, which can help increase the confidence and sense of effectiveness in the world. This should not be solely about control, but more about seeing oneself as a part of something bigger which is not something to be afraid of but helps individuals to address and meet their needs and wants.

Experiencing the World

Psychosis often leads to a vicious cycle which leads to less rather than more communication. Anxieties and a changed perception of reality can lead to a disengagement from it, which reduces the ability to distinguish internal from external reality even more.

Identifying Meaning in the World

To break through the vicious cycle of anxiety, in which emotions like fear and anxiety cause a withdrawal into the internal world, which in turn reinforce feelings of fear, loneliness, sadness, and so forth, it is helpful to focus on identifying what is meaningful and having more of it in life. Communication helps in identifying and finding meaning, either communication with oneself or with others. The exchange of messages is like a learning process in which meaning can be identified, found and accumulated. Through meaningful interactions one accumulates more meaning, more connectedness with oneself and the world and reduces the need for thoughts and behaviors which are triggered by fears, guilt, self-blame and other negative emotions. This also helps against depression and anxiety.

Increasing Interactions

Perceiving more meaning also makes interacting with others and oneself more meaningful. This has a positive effect on one's interaction patterns, how and in which one ways one relates to one's environment and exchanges messages with it. As the anxiety about interactions with others decreases, it should become easier to become more socially involved with others, at least to the extent which would feel comfortable to the individual also without the illness.

Values, Needs and Aspirations

Often, individuals suffering from anxiety or burnout have become uncertain about what is really important to them and the fit between these values and interests and their current life situation. Whether in the professional or romantic realms, getting what one needs and values makes happy in the long run, everything else does not. If I value helping people, it is important that I do that to make me happy. At the same time, I might value time spent with friend and spending time by myself. It is important that I can do this in the long run, because otherwise I will not be as happy as I could be.

Meaningful Messages as the Instrument of Change

Communication is the vehicle of change. The instruments are meaningful messages which are generated and received by the people who take part in these interactions. In a therapeutic setting, keeping the mutual flow of information relevant and meaningful brings change in both people who take part in this process. The learning curve for the patient may be steeper in certain respects because he or she spends less time in this interaction style than a therapist.

Knowing Where Information Comes From

In the end, the patent should have a better sense of communicating and knowing where information comes from. This helps build a stronger sense of self but also imparts confidence in dealing with everyday life as well towards fulfilling own aspirations.

Posttraumatic Stress Disorder (PTSD)

Introduction

Post-traumatic stress disorder (PTSD) is the result of an event that is not supposed to occur, whether a tropical storm or a rape. They also take one outside the usual human experience. The link between oneself and the world seems to be severed. Reality has changed in how it feels and in what it seems.

Reconnecting

The goal is to reconnect with oneself and with the world. The tool to accomplish this is through communication, which can be the interaction in psychotherapy, for example. It happens in the space of a meaningful relationship.

Safety and Certainty

When something has happened, which is not supposed to happen, it seems a formidable task to get the patient used to the fact that what happened has been a statistical outlier, something that usually does not happen in this world. Since some of the most severe traumata happen on the interpersonal level, through exchanging meaning, including individual perspectives and values, in therapy, the patient can again get a better sense of faith in other human beings.

Psychodynamic Psychotherapy and CBT

Both of these therapies have shown effectiveness in the treatment of PTSD. Both have theories about why they help. The former sees learning processes about certain thought processes as central, the latter psychodynamic processes that bring about a change. However, they both neglect the communication process and changes in how people communicate as what ultimately helps. The difference to interpersonal psychotherapy is that the latter focuses more on the interpersonal setting than the actual communication processes.

The tool that helps in the end is the communication between therapist and patient which can bring about change through the meaningful messages that are exchange in it. This is why focusing on communication in the first place, can help bring about deeper and lasting change.

Insight

Within the meaningful interactions of therapist and patients, or in any other relevant setting, if it s working well, relevant messages are generated which have the power to bring about change. Messages can bring about change if the recipient regards it as relevant and it contains some new information. The processing of this new information adds something to the recipient, even if the content is rejected as false. In other words, every meaningful interaction gets us further, helps us develop insight into ourselves and the world.

Especially in the case of PTSD, this insight is relevant because it makes the world predictable again. One may not understand why the hurricane hit this specific village or why a parent was abusive, but to realize that how such horrible experiences are processes has a certain course and is predictable, makes the world a better place again.

Source of the Problem

The therapeutic setting should also make it easier to determine in a safe environment that the person with issues is not the victim, but the perpetrator, if there is one. If one has fallen victim to a natural disaster, it still helps to find out more about these kinds of disasters. Again, insight into the problem can be helpful, because it shifts the focus away from self-blame, feeling guilt or other unhelpful emotions.

Understanding PTSD

The trauma is highly personal. Some people may interpret something as a trauma, which others do not. Much depends on one's outlook on life and one's past experiences. It is highly subjective. However, in many extreme situations, it is unlikely that there is no traumatization in even the most resilient person. Rape or torture in the vast majority of cases cause symptoms of PTSD, sometimes with a substantial delay of years or even decades.

The Trauma

Trauma does not require physical harm or wounds. Rape, for example, does not have to leave physical scars, but it usually does leave psychological ones. To understand trauma, one needs to understand that physical integrity is usually complimented by psychological integrity, a sense of self and person which is a whole and deserves respect as such. Communication can be used as a weapon to inflict great psychological harm.

Often, there are already maladaptive communication patterns before, that cause the problems in the relationship or interpersonal interactions. These patterns can be analyzed and changed. Another important element is that communication can also take place on the inside of the individual.

Uncertainty

In life, one has to live with uncertainty. Uncertainty just means that there is no manual in the beginning and there are still unknowns which leave room for excitement and exploration. Life is a learning experience. An individual suffering from anxiety may have areas in life where she thrives on excitement, and other areas where images of worst case scenarios cause her to freeze when she just considers a change in action or any action at all. Uncertainty to someone suffering from anxiety seems to be bearable in some areas and avoided in others. Often, the areas where it is not tolerated feel meaningful only to the person suffering from anxiety.

Communication Deficits

Areas which people often feel anxious about are where there has been an issue with their interpersonal interactions in the past. Early traumata, like a disappearing or abusive parent, stay unresolved. For example, if a parent feels fearful and angry with himself and this is picked up by a child, the latter may decode these messages correctly in that the parent is angry, but since the parent may not be conscious about it, the child does not pick up on the second important half of the message, that the parent has a problem with himself and his issue is unrelated to the child. Of course, one can learn to pick up on the self-blame and frustration of the parent, and therapists should become experts at reading between the lines in this fashion, but it requires experience, reflection and insight into transference and counter-transference phenomena, for example, to use the psychoanalytic terms.

Avoidance

Anxiety can lead to avoidance, which in turn can attach even more anxiety to the situations or behaviors which are being avoided. In social situations, not interacting with others deprives the person of continuously updating and honing the skills and confidence of interacting with others. Avoidance can thus lead to an increase rather than a decrease in anxiety in the long-run.

Meaning

Individuals suffering from anxiety and panic attacks often see less meaning in the things they do. In therapy an important part is to rediscover meaning and find it in the things that are relevant to the patient. Relevant is anything that is close to his or her values, basic interests, aspirations, wants, wishes and desires.

An important step in therapy thus to make the person aware of how anxiety affects one's thinking. Individuals from anxiety often focus differently from other individuals. There is often a focus on worst outcomes and strong fears which are caused by it. Underlying this are often strong emotions or conflicts which need to be defended against. The danger and uncertainty is quite frequently inside oneself, rather than on the outside. An individual with a fear of flying may be more afraid of not containing oneself and not being able to leave the plain than anything else. Anxiety is the fear of crashing oneself and the feelings of a dreaded uncertainty about oneself and one's emotional states.

Meaning of the Trauma

If something bad happens, one may say that it does not have meaning. But it is relevant to the individual and changed the course of events, and communication may have played a role. So, there is probably some meaning to it. The important element is that it needs to be seen subjectively from within the life of the person affected by it.

Integration of the Meaning into the Sense of Self

The important next step is to integrate the effect it has on the individual into the individual's sense of self. In the case of the hurricane, it may be that one is sad and angry about the loss of a loved one, but that hurricanes, storms, and the changing weather itself, is a part of a dynamic changing world in which one lives as a human being. No one has control over the weather, and at least at the present accepting this just means that one also has no responsibility over it.

Experiencing the World

To break through the vicious cycle of anxiety, in which emotions like fear and anxiety cause safety thoughts and behaviors, which in turn reinforce feelings of fear, loneliness, sadness, and so forth, it is helpful to focus on identifying what is meaningful and having more of it in life. Communication helps in identifying and finding meaning, either communication with oneself or with others. The exchange of messages is like a learning process in which meaning can be identified, found and accumulated. Through meaningful interactions one accumulates more meaning, more connectedness with oneself and the world and reduces the need for thoughts and behaviors which are triggered by fears, guilt, self-blame and other negative emotions. This also helps against depression and anxiety.

Perceiving more meaning also makes interacting with others and oneself more meaningful. This has a positive effect on one's interaction patterns, how and in which one ways one relates to one's environment and exchanges messages with it.

Change

A trauma has the power to change how one experiences the world, even though one wished for this change. However, one has a choice over the flavor of this change, whether it changes the meaning one gives to aspects of the world. In the best case scenario, one may even see more in the world, more meaning, than before. At a minimum, therapy should make it possible to exchange information about the meaning aspects of the trauma have to the person and be understood by the therapist. If the therapist does not understand a particular piece, he or she should ask to get at least a good sense for it to be able to engage in the process which ultimately creates new meaning through the exchange of meaningful messages.

Values, Needs and Aspirations

Often, individuals suffering from anxiety or burnout have become uncertain about what is really important to them and the fit between these values and interests and their current life situation. Whether in the professional or romantic realms, getting what one needs and values makes happy in the long run, everything else does not. If I value helping people, it is important that I do that to make me happy. At the same time, I might value time spent with friend and spending time by myself. It is important that I can do this in the long run, because otherwise I will not be as happy as I could be.

Meaningful Messages as the Instrument of Change

Communication is the vehicle of change. The instruments are meaningful messages which are generated and received by the people who take part in these interactions. In a therapeutic setting, keeping the mutual flow of information relevant and meaningful brings change in both people who take part in this process. The learning curve for the patient may be steeper in certain respects

because he or she spends less time in this interaction style than a therapist.

Maintaining the Communication Process

The process through which change can occur in many cases runs automatically. However, a therapeutic setting can get more out of it then if one just waits enough time. Also, in a number of cases people get stuck in the PTSD. The reason for this is that it requires meaningful communication for the process, and if one becomes afraid of it or does not believe in it, constructive and dynamic communication can effectively shut down. A therapist should provide a setting that feels safe enough to engage in the process but be inquisitive and active enough to move the process along if there are resistance points coming up, whether in the patient or the therapist. In any instance, the therapist should be alert, thoughtful, reflecting, be able to take a view from a distance, and be empathetic.

New Meaning and Integration

The construction of new meaning and the integration of this into one's sense of self is one of the primary goals of the therapy of PTSD. This also includes addressing, resolving and integrating emotions into the self in a meaningful way. The end result should make the trauma an event in the past, whose story is integrated into the much larger story of the individual.

Schizophrenia

Introduction

Schizophrenia is a condition of the brain in which the internal and outside worlds become difficult to distinguish. Internal thoughts or emotions become external voices or threatening forces, or outside events or things are felt to have direct effect on one's own thoughts and sense of self. This thinning of the border between outside and inside worlds can have a number of biological and psychological reasons, yet what it comes down to is that the flow of information, communication inside the brain or between it and the outside world is interpreted differently.

One way to treat this condition is therefore with the help of communication, such as takes place in a therapeutic setting. Reflecting on and interpreting messages helps to regain the tools to be able to draw these boundaries again.

Schizophrenia

Schizophrenia is a mental disorder characterized by abnormal social behavior and failure to understand what is real. This seems to affect both, the internal and external worlds of the patient. Communication can no longer be identified as being clearly in the external world or in the internal world. Common symptoms include false beliefs, unclear or confused thinking, hearing voices that others do not hear, reduced social engagement and emotional expression, and a lack of motivation. People with schizophrenia often have additional mental health problems such as anxiety, depressive, or substance-use disorders. Symptoms typically come on gradually, begin in young adulthood, and can last a long time.

The causes of schizophrenia include environmental and genetic factors. Possible environmental factors include being raised in a city, cannabis use during adolescence, certain infections, parental age and poor nutrition during pregnancy. Genetic factors include a variety of common and rare genetic variants.

About one in two hundred people are affected by schizophrenia during their lifetimes. Males are more often affected than females. Social problems, such as long-term unemployment, poverty and homelessness are common. The average life expectancy of people with the disorder is ten to twenty-five years less than for the general population.

Understanding Schizophrenia

The localization where the source of information is located seems impeded. This probably leads to some of the more common symptoms in schizophrenia. Also, this can lead to anxiety and fears because when one misinterprets the sources of information being received it changes reality and can make it frightening and scary.

Weakness of the Inside-Outside Divide

Information from inside and outside is processed in the brain often side by side. There is only one brain. The information itself is similar, whether one is thinking of touching a cat or actually doing so, and the brain has to be able whether something is communicated from the outside or from the inside. In people with schizophrenia this does not seem to work as it does in others without the condition.

Anything that helps to support the brain functions which make the distinction can be useful in treating schizophrenia.

Uncommunicated Emotions

Paranoid thoughts, that one is pursued or watched, often lead to fear, which can cause the agitation and panic in some patients. The problem is that emotions, such as anger or fear cannot be communicated effectively, and then become manifest if the division between the inside and outside world is not stable enough.

Loss of Contact with Oneself and Others

The dynamics of the illness as well as the consequences of the symptoms often lead to loss of contact with oneself and others. The breakdown in the distinction of whether information comes from inside or outside the body also leads to a loss of self as the entity where one's thoughts originate from. As the sense of self gets lost, the patient can no longer communicate with oneself. This then can lead to existential fears, loss of confidence and a breakdown in the internal coherence of various mental functions and perceptions. The end result is that the patient is confronted with a void, an emptiness, into which he is afraid to disappear, leading to extreme fears, and in some cases behaviors.

The loss of contact with others is a result of losing contact with oneself. If communication with oneself is no longer possible, neither is a meaningful interaction with the outside world. As the inside world ceases to exist, the outside world does so as well. One cannot be without the other.

What is left is a large unstructured and frightening space in which fragments of thoughts and emotions drift without interacting with each other in a coherent way. As the outside and inside break down, so do the rules of flows of information, and the communication between points becomes unpredictable and frightening.

Experiencing the World

To break through the vicious cycle of anxiety, in which emotions like fear and anxiety cause safety thoughts and behaviors, which in turn reinforce feelings of fear, loneliness, sadness, and so forth, it is helpful to focus on identifying what is meaningful and having more of it in life. Communication helps in identifying and finding meaning, either communication with oneself or with others. The exchange of messages is like a learning process in which meaning can be identified, found and accumulated. Through meaningful interactions one accumulates more meaning, more connectedness with oneself and the world and reduces the need for thoughts and behaviors which are triggered by fears, guilt, self-blame and other negative emotions. This also helps against depression and anxiety.

Making the World Meaningful Again

Perceiving more meaning also makes interacting with others and oneself more meaningful. This has a positive effect on one's interaction patterns, how and in which one ways one relates to one's environment and exchanges messages with it.

Communication as a Structuring Process

Engaging in the communication process can help give the patient a sense of structure also with a view to other processes and mechanisms. Learning about communication, but importantly also engaging in it, helps the patient to acquire a sense of internal structure between mental processes and entities. As the sense of self s rebuilt, a meaningful communication between the inside and the outside can commence again.

Values, Needs and Aspirations

Often, individuals suffering from anxiety or burnout have become uncertain about what is really important to them and the fit between these values and interests and their current life situation. Whether in the professional or romantic realms, getting what one needs and values makes happy in the long run, everything else does not. If I value helping people, it is important that I do that to make me happy.

At the same time, I might value time spent with friend and spending time by myself. It is important that I can do this in the long run, because otherwise I will not be as happy as I could be.

Meaningful Messages as the Instrument of Change

Communication is the vehicle of change. The instruments are meaningful messages which are generated and received by the people who take part in these interactions. In a therapeutic setting, keeping the mutual flow of information relevant and meaningful brings change in both people who take part in this process. The learning curve for the patient may be steeper in certain respects because he or she spends less time in this interaction style than a therapist.

Sexual Disorders

Introduction

Sexual disorder is difficulty experienced by an individual or a couple during any stage of a normal sexual activity, including physical pleasure, desire, preference, arousal or orgasm. In the following, the psychological side of sexual disorders. It is important in this regard to see sexuality also as a form of communication which contains the exchange of various messages. Problems in communication often lead to sexual dysfunctions. Openness and a willingness to receive meaningful messages can be found in human sexuality.

Dealing with problems in the sexual area does not only require openness and a greater willingness to communicate, but also to reflect and improve on the interactions people have with themselves and among them in a relationship. Sex is very private because it relates   to organs that have a function with enormous effects, procreation, even if they are not used for that purpose. They also distinguish people in a very fundamental biological way.

Communication links people together if they exchange meaningful messages, which can include stroking someone's hair, for example. A sexual interaction actually means a lot of communication on many communication channels. Even procreative sexual intercourse is communication as information is transferred in the form of DNA. It is important to appreciate the enormous role communication plays to effectively treat sexual disorders. To get partners to communicate meaningfully about it with each other is one objective of the treatment of difficulties around sex.

Sexual Disorders

Sexual disorders can largely be group into the following categories: sexual desire disorders, arousal disorders, orgasm disorders and pain disorders. Especially the former have a significant psychological component. Anxieties, self-image and the ability to engage in a close and intimate dialogue with another human being can all play a role.

Communication with Oneself

The way one communicates with oneself, one's dreams and mental images, have a profound effect on one's sexuality and ability to engage in a sexual interaction with another human being, where this can include anything from flirtatious behavior to penetrative sex. Since sex is a form of communication, looking at it from a communication perspective is helpful.

Communicating with the Partner

To understand the communication patterns, but also the needs and aspirations, of the partners in their interactions is an important key in treating sexual disorders. Total silence is usually a worse prognostic indicator than heated emotional arguments, because in the latter there is at least still an emotional exchange in some form. Often there is a partial silence, meaning that the partners may be afraid or feel other, maybe even strong, emotions about the topic. As long as the issue seems relevant, the therapeutic process should cover it at some point.

Difficult issues

In many cases, it may be better to start with the low anxiety issues and then move up to the more anxiety inducing ones, such as general questions about children or even the general direction of the relationship, but not in all. Sometimes it is impossible to get effective work done without addressing a particular issue.

Meaning of Relationship

It is important for the partners to be able to formulate the meaning they attach to relationship in general. Only if both know what they want and need in a relationship, what their desires, aspirations and values are, is it possible to consider change in the relationship. One has to know the direction of the journey to be able to decide on the next turn. This can require that the partners work individually with a therapist to find answers to this question. It can require going back in time and reflecting on past relationships and to become clearer about one's values and fundamental needs and wants by taking stock of what truly feels good and what does not. In many cases, this may require dealing with other issues that make it difficult to connect with one's own emotions and make them less accessible.

Meaning of the Current Relationship

Once the partner's needs and expectations for a relationship in general have been explored, it is important to reflect on the current relationship. What does each get or does not get in the relationship and what they feel they are each contributing. The important point is to communicate about, so that each gets a sense that the other understands. Understanding reduces anxiety and the pressure each of them might experience, which can significantly contribute to sexual problems and dysfunctions.

Communicating through the Body

Humans communicate through their bodies, where speech is only one possible communication channel. The vast majority of information that is sent and received between intimate partners is non-verbal. This communication can be highly meaningful and also needs to be practiced. Touching another is also communicating information and it can be meaningful, just as saying something. Messages do not have to be highly complex to be meaningful, often simpler ones can be quite effective. On the other hand, there is probably an infinite variety in touching someone in regard to how, where, and so on. Becoming more sensitive and literate in sending messages through the body is an important step in reducing many problems of intimacy and sexuality. People may, for example, be afraid of how a message will be received, but that goes back to little experience in focusing on communication inquisitively, and seeing it as a tool that can be managed, rather than being managed by it.

Understanding Sexual Disorders

Fears and anxiety, which can stem from past life experiences, often interfere with one's communication with oneself and others because when we interact with others we can feel at our most vulnerable, a vulnerability which can be even higher in a sexual interaction.

Vulnerability

A vulnerability predisposes an individual to problems in the face of specific stressors. Psychological vulnerabilities can be thoughts that trigger certain emotions or certain beliefs about oneself or others. They usually stem from a person's past experiences, or more specifically, what an individual has learned about how communication works and the effects it has. Abusive messages can lead to a thought of being punished for something, but the important determinant of the future vulnerability is the own reaction to the message. If talking back to establish boundaries make the abusive situation only worse, one fails to draw boundaries in future, which in a relationship situation may mean one cannot talk about one's emotions out of fear that this only makes things worse. The result is than a partial, or full, silence which places a burden on the relationship.

Shame and Guilt

Resolving these fears and anxieties can be facilitated in a safe and open environment, where one can speak easily about very personal thoughts and emotions. In therapy, this means that the therapist should listen and work with questions that clarify and reflect rather than outwardly probe. After all, the topics can be very private and associated with shame, or even guilt.

Shame and guilt can best be dealt with in the interaction with another human being where a meaningful exchange and a reflection about it is possible. Feedback is an important part of it because shame and guilt are often a result of not enough feedback.

Novelty and Creativity

It is also important to appreciate that sexual interactions thrive on novelty and creativeness, or excitement. Anxiety can reduce one's ability to be creative and innovative, and express it. Training with the patient better patterns of communication, which are less anxiety-provoking, can lead to greater openness and willingness to experiment.

Meaning

Sexuality can have various sources of meaning. It makes happy, in some cases leads to procreation and the survival of the human species, and the interaction itself can help improve both partners personality and sense of self. Relevant is anything that is close to his or her values, basic interests, aspirations, wants, wishes and desires.

An important step in therapy thus to make the person aware of how anxiety affects one's thinking. Individuals from anxiety often focus differently from other individuals. There is often a focus on worst outcomes and strong fears which are caused by it. Underlying this are often strong emotions or conflicts which need to be defended against. The danger and uncertainty is quite frequently inside oneself, rather than on the outside. An individual with a fear of flying may be more afraid of not containing oneself and not being able to leave the plain than anything else. Anxiety is the fear of crashing oneself and the feelings of a dreaded uncertainty about oneself and one's emotional states.

Sexual Purpose

Sex in a biological context has recreation as its purpose. However, reducing it just to this theme belies that sexuality is communication on many different channels. As living organisms we interact and exchange messages with others like us or different from us. In the process, we learn more about ourselves, as in an intense sexual interaction, a lot of communication takes place with ourselves and others around us. The important step is to see this vast amount of communication, appreciate it and be able to reflect on it.

The Sense of Self

Our exchange of meaningful messages with others and with ourselves shapes our sense of self to a large degree. The emotions are also messages which are communicated within one's body and inform the sense one has of oneself. During a sexual interaction, unless one tries to block it to a large degree, there is an intensive exchange of information on the inside and on the outside, including in the form of emotions, which can thus have an enormous impact on one's sense of self.

Creativity and Excitement

Information has meaning if it is relevant to and can be understood by the person receiving it. Usually there also has to be something novel in a message which is meaningful, because if something has meaning it brings about a change in the individual's perspective of oneself or the world around. The ability to create meaning can thus lead to excitement in the other person, and in oneself. Intense interactions, such as sexual communication, are built and maintained more easily if there is creativity about it.

Experiencing the World

To break through the vicious cycle of anxiety, in which emotions like fear and anxiety cause safety thoughts and behaviors, which in turn reinforce feelings of fear, loneliness, sadness, and so forth, it is helpful to focus on identifying what is meaningful and having more of it in life. Communication helps in identifying and finding meaning, either communication with oneself or with others. The exchange of messages is like a learning process in which meaning can be identified, found and accumulated. Through meaningful interactions one accumulates more meaning, more connectedness with oneself and the world and reduces the need for thoughts and behaviors which are triggered by fears, guilt, self-blame and other negative emotions. This also helps against depression and anxiety.

Perceiving more meaning also makes interacting with others and oneself more meaningful. This has a positive effect on one's interaction patterns, how and in which one ways one relates to one's environment and exchanges messages with it.

Values, Needs and Aspirations

Often, individuals suffering from anxiety or burnout have become uncertain about what is really important to them and the fit between these values and interests and their current life situation. Whether in the professional or romantic realms, getting what one needs and values makes happy in the long run, everything else does not. If I value helping people, it is important that I do that to make me happy. At the same time, I might value time spent with friend and spending time by myself. It is important that I can do this in the long run, because otherwise I will not be as happy as I could be.

Meaningful Messages as the Instrument of Change

Communication is the vehicle of change. The instruments are meaningful messages which are generated and received by the people who take part in these interactions. In a therapeutic setting, keeping the mutual flow of information relevant and meaningful brings change in both people who take part in this process. The learning curve for the patient may be steeper in certain respects because he or she spends less time in this interaction style than a therapist.

Social Anxiety and Shyness

Introduction

Social anxiety is quite common. 90% will have experienced an episode of social anxiety in their lives. However, if it occurs early and over a prolonged period of time, it can interfere with a person's mate selection, school work, education and the job he or she chooses. This form of anxiety may be one of the most problematic ones, because it may still be possible to do school work, find a job and find a partner, but there will always be the feeling that one could have done better.

Basically, social anxiety is a form of anxiety. This means that there is an element of uncertainty and a sense that something in life is out of sync. Unfortunately, it affects the system where an autoregulation could take place, communication.

Social Anxiety and Shyness

Social anxiety can be defined as nervousness in social situations. What is meant by 'social situations' is a situation where communication takes place among a number of people or in front of people. It is rarer that it affects people in one-on-one interactions.

Some of it may be related to not have a sense of control or to make the other more powerful, important or relevant, which could judge oneself.

Symptoms

Individuals higher in social anxiety avert their gazes, show fewer facial expressions, and show difficulty with initiating and maintaining conversation. Trait social anxiety, the stable tendency to experience this nervousness, can be distinguished from state anxiety, the momentary response to a particular social stimulus. Nearly 90% of individuals report feeling a form of social anxiety (i.e., shyness) at some point in their lives. Half of the individuals with any social fears meet criteria for social anxiety disorder. The function of social anxiety is to increase arousal and attention to social interactions, inhibit unwanted social behavior, and motivate preparation for social situations such as performance situations.

Projection

Projecting one's own thought into the other is a common mechanism which contrbvutes to social anxiety. It means that one is, for example, critical of oneself and then sees this in the audience or other people. Everyone is than as critical of the own person as oneself. Often, just realizing what is happening can resolve a good deal of the social anxiety.

Co-Morbidity

Some disorders associated with the social anxiety spectrum include anxiety disorders, mood disorders, autism, eating disorders, and substance use disorders. Unfortunately, this means that the process which can contribute largely to getting better is affected by it.

Understanding Social Anxiety and Shyness

Social anxiety is often present from childhood. The fears already interfere wuth one's development early on. Since some of the most experiences in a human life are the interpersonal ones, this can interfere with one's personal development. As already mentioned, shyness is not a disorder, and a person may be happy about it. However, the potential loss to quality of life of social anxiety and shyness can be similar. Shy people often develop adaptive communication pathways, such as relying more heavily on the Internet and may be content with it. However, interpersonal communication is an important piece of change and of bringing about in the world, and without it some of this dynamic may be missed out on.

Internal Communication

Often, there are already maladaptive communication patterns before, that cause the problems in the relationship or interpersonal interactions. These patterns can be analyzed and changed. Another important element is that communication can also take place on the inside of the individual. Individuals with social anxiety are often very critical of themselves, and this is what is then projected into others, who then appear critical of oneself. An important, and often helpful, step is

Uncertainty

In life, one has to live with uncertainty. Uncertainty just means that there is no manual in the beginning and there are still unknowns which leave room for excitement and exploration. Life is a learning experience. An individual suffering from anxiety may have areas in life where she thrives on excitement, and other areas where images of worst case scenarios cause her to freeze when she just considers a change in action or any action at all. Uncertainty to someone suffering from anxiety seems to be bearable in some areas and avoided in others. Often, the areas where it is not tolerated feel meaningful only to the person suffering from anxiety.

Communication Deficits

Areas which people often feel anxious about are where there has been an issue with their interpersonal interactions in the past. Early traumata, like a disappearing or abusive parent, stay unresolved. For example, if a parent feels fearful and angry with himself and this is picked up by a child, the latter may decode these messages correctly in that the parent is angry, but since the parent may not be conscious about it, the child does not pick up on the second important half of the message, that the parent has a problem with himself and his issue is unrelated to the child. Of course, one can learn to pick up on the self-blame and frustration of the parent, and therapists should become experts at reading between the lines in this fashion, but it requires experience, reflection and insight into transference and counter-transference phenomena, for example, to use the psychoanalytic terms.

Avoidance

Anxiety can lead to avoidance, which in turn can attach even more anxiety to the situations or behaviors which are being avoided. In social situations, not interacting with others deprives the person of continuously updating and honing the skills and confidence of interacting with others. Avoidance can thus lead to an increase rather than a decrease in anxiety in the long-run.

Meaning

Individuals suffering from social anxiety do not see less relevance in social interactions, but often even more. They often interpret messages in a way that goes beyond what someone without social anxiety may do. However, while the patient with social anxiety may give the interaction too much relevance in relation to her self-image or an important need or value, she may actually see less details in t than someone else. The fear of an interaction is often the result of an acknowledgment on a subconscious level that one may not have enough information or not understand enough to make an interaction successful and enjoyable.

The therapeutic session should help the patient to gain the skills and insight and skills to see more in interactions with other people and find it easier to focus on what is meaningful and relevant. This often means becoming better at filtering out information and developing a sense for what is not relevant to oneself. This usually requires that the patient first assesses his or her basic parameters (values, needs and aspirations) to have a better idea which communication styles to adopt and what to look out for.

Awareness of Thought Patterns

An important step in therapy thus to make the person aware of how anxiety affects one's thinking. Individuals from anxiety often focus differently from other individuals. There is often a focus on worst outcomes and strong fears which are caused by it. Underlying this are often strong emotions or conflicts which need to be defended against. The danger and uncertainty is quite frequently inside oneself, rather than on the outside. An individual with a fear of flying may be more afraid of not containing oneself and not being able to leave the plain than anything else. Anxiety is the fear of crashing oneself and the feelings of a dreaded uncertainty about oneself and one's emotional states.

Emotional Substrate

If there have been adverse life experiences as a significant factor in the social anxiety, there can still be unresolved emotions underlying the anxiety. To resolve them means answering the hypothetical question, what one may have felt in the difficult situation, but then also seeing the strength that allowed one to pull through, which only becomes visible now. The goal is not necessarily to reconnect with only negative emotions form the past, but also the good ones, and emotions as a whole today.

Experiencing the World

Social anxiety means potentially experiencing less of the world, although the higher sensitivity can at the same time let someone experience more. High sensitivity is not a bad, but the capability to perceive and experience more about oneself and the world. The important part is to make it work for one, rather than feeling constrained by it.

Communication Techniques

Various communication techniques can be helpful, not as an end in themselves, but to help the person have more confidence in oneself and to see communication not as something dangerous one needs to be guarded against, but as something that can help one meet one's needs, wishes and expectations. Thus, the reason for communication techniques should be not an end in itself, but to increase one's repertoire, ease and confidence in communicating with oneself and others.

Breaking the Cycle of Anxiety

To break through the vicious cycle of anxiety, in which emotions like fear and anxiety cause safety thoughts and behaviors, which in turn reinforce feelings of fear, loneliness, sadness, and so forth, it is helpful to focus on identifying what is meaningful and having more of it in life. Communication helps in identifying and finding meaning, either communication with oneself or with others. The exchange of messages is like a learning process in which meaning can be identified, found and accumulated. Through meaningful interactions one accumulates more meaning, more connectedness with oneself and the world and reduces the need for thoughts and behaviors which are triggered by fears, guilt, self-blame and other negative emotions. This also helps against depression and anxiety.

The Reward of Seeing More

Perceiving more meaning also makes interacting with others and oneself more meaningful. This has a positive effect on one's interaction patterns, how and in which one ways one relates to one's environment and exchanges messages with it.

Values, Needs and Aspirations

As already mentioned, these are the basic parameters which do not change much over time and which many people feel define them to a certain degree. This is also why they exert a considerable influence on a person's self-image and, by extension, on the anxiety level.

The main difficulty in social anxiety is not that the basic parameters are 'wrong', but that one has difficulties reading them and identifying with them. This leads to a situation where the compass and a clear sense of direction is missing. Individuals with social anxiety often have a predisposition for heightened anxiety levels, but they are also missing the groundedness and clarity of purpose someone else might have. It is thus important to help the patient find the compass needle again, which not only helps in cases of social anxiety, but life in general.

The Need for Communication

Living organisms have a need for communicating with themselves and others. This is needed to grow, innovate and propagate. Most of the human accomplishments in the arts, sciences and professions are based on the exchange of meaningful messages, communication. But communication is also to have one's needs met and to survive in general. Even a hermit in the mountains needs to interact with his or her living mountain environment. People who enjoy nature usually do not want to shun communication but focus on an exchange with a nonhuman environment. Communication is fundamental to life itself.

It often helps people with social anxiety and shyness to connect with and appreciate their need and joy in communicating. Once communication is seen as a potential source of joy rather than a necessary task, it can become much easier, as 'I want' replaces 'I should'.

Meaningful Messages as the Instrument of Change

Communication is the vehicle of change. The instruments are meaningful messages which are generated and received by the people who take part in these interactions. In a therapeutic setting, keeping the mutual flow of information relevant and meaningful brings change in both people who take part in this process. The learning curve for the patient may be steeper in certain respects because he or she spends less time in this interaction style than a therapist.

Embracing Change

In social anxiety, embracing change can be associated with anxiety, but it can also be liberating, because it means that there are no rigid rules one needs to adhere to other than those linked to the communication process itself, which has clear laws. Understanding these laws of communication, on the other hand, which humans subconsciously operate on and use as they accumulate experience in their interactions with others is important to be more confident in tolerating and working towards change. Basic communication concepts, such as what constitutes communication, how meaning is created, how information flows, and how communication processes are influenced, is usually not conscious, but reflecting on it and beginning to use it can be especially helpful to sensitive people, who quite frequently have experienced social at some point in their lives. One might say, that only those who do not care about people and themselves are entirely free from social anxiety.

Psychotherapeutic Technique: A Brief Overview

Introduction

When patients come to see a therapist, they often have a long list of things that do not work for them in their lives. It is easy to overlook that one of the hardest steps towards health has been taken, stepping into the office of a therapist. Psychotherapeutic Technique is then largely about helping the patient find his or her path and to have the courage to follow it. Empathy, common sense, and a good dose of optimism are helpful in this line of work, as is thinking about what is happening and has happened in the life of the patient, how they relate to themselves and the world, and that in the end everything should make sense to the head and to the heart.

The reasoning mind plays a greater role in psychotherapy than it is given credit for. Many mental health conditions arise because of what we think we have to achieve, because we think there are no alternative options or because we think we have failed. If one's thoughts can make one feel worse, it also makes sense to look to one's thoughts to make oneself feel better. However, the goal is not to engage in endless loops of thinking about unanswerable questions but to engage with one's thoughts by asking whether they make sense or not.

The author has developed communication-focused therapy (CFT) out of the need for an approach which addresses more directly the processes which underlie most psychotherapeutic approaches. (1) It tries to address some of the shortcomings of cognitive behavioral therapy (CBT) and psychodynamic therapy, as well as those of others.

Communication

Communication is the foundation of any change processes in life, including psychotherapy. (1)   Meaningful messages contain the information which brings about change in the recipient, and quite often also in the sender of the message. In order to bring about change, the recipient of it must be able to decode it, and it must resonate with him or her. This usually requires also that the information has a degree of novelty.

The author has developed communication-focused therapy to focus on this fundamental process and developed applications for several mental health conditions, including depression (2), anxiety (3), social anxiety (4), OCD (5), psychosis (6), eating disorder, ADHD, and several others. Some of the techniques may not be entirely new, but the perspective is to the author's knowledge new.

Making Sense

In the best-case scenario, a patient engages in a process of 'making sense' with the help of the therapist. This does not just mean using logic but seeing one's thoughts within the context of one's values and aspirations on one side, and one's experiences and interactions with other people on the other side. In the end, the objectives and goals of one's thoughts have to make sense within the context of one's values. This ultimately leads to stable and persistent happiness and mental well-being.

Let us look at an example, which applies to many people. If one of my values is to provide a safe environment for my family, thinking about how to make more money can lead to greater happiness (and less stress), if I am aware that I am thinking about earning money to be able to buy a house that can offer my family a greater sense of security. If I see money as an end in itself, on the other hand, it can lead to an obsession, which may become endless, because I lose sight of when I have reached my goal.

In other words, life becomes easier once we see our actions and interactions with other people as something that ultimately makes sense for us. One does not need to have a specific outcome in mind. A feeling of significance to oneself is already a good starting point. Many people lack even this general feeling in most of their daily lives, which can lead to emotional disengagement, burnout, depression anxiety, panic attacks, heightened OCD, and so forth. Therapy has to bring 'sense' and meaning into the equation again.

The Coherent Sense of Self

In order for the world to make sense, oneself has to make sense. Individuals look for messages or information that they hope gives them a sense of 'wholeness'. This can come from inside or outside themselves, and it is closely aligned with the need for self-actualization and the quest for the happiness which is brought by fulfilling one's true needs, values and aspirations. What binds everything together is information.

Guided Self-Help

Much of what can happen in therapy depends on the expectations of the patient. It determines how much he or she will participate in therapy and contribute to the process in general. This makes it worthwhile to point out early to the basic working in principle in therapy, that the therapist can help patients help themselves, but should under normal circumstances not tell them what to do.

The Search for Meaning

Therapy is about meaning, helping a patient find relevance in things, which also asks patients to look at their fundamental values and basic interests. Following one's values and basic interests leads to happiness and not knowing them to such conditions as anxiety and burnout. Many people in today's busy and increasingly complex world lose their ability to see relevance in the world and in what they do. Helping people to reconnect the world as they perceive it with what they value is an important aspect of therapy. It requires the ability to communicate with oneself and between the inside and outside worlds.

The Therapeutic Relationship

Therapy is an exchange of information, which ultimately should help the patient to lead a happier and more fulfilling life, as well as be free from any symptoms that interfere with these goals. The motivation for it should come for a need for the feedback and information that is provided in therapy. The therapeutic relationship is the bundle of channels along which the therapeutic communication takes place.

Observation

The therapist should be able to see how patients deal with information and interact with themselves and the world around them. Better communication with oneself and others can lead to the patient feeling safer, developing greater abilities of introspection and reflection and facilitating a healthier communication with oneself and the environment. All this requires that the therapist has an understanding of the dynamics of interactions in general and of the interactions of the patient in specific, the mutual flow of information and the values, aspirations and interests everyone holds.

Empathy and Interest

Therapeutic work requires empathy and an honest and true interest in the patient and his or her inner worlds. The therapist should also have an interest for the own inner worlds and how they are are influenced by the communication of the patient. In psychoanalysis, the concepts of transference and counter-transference are used here.

Reason

Mostly therapy is about leading the patient with questions and comments to find new perspectives, open up to new information and process information in new ways. The epiphanies should take place in the patient, while the therapist can create the setting in which they take place. The motivation, ownership and integration into the own person that takes place in them is important for the success of therapy.

Values, Interests and Aspirations

The psychodynamic process helps to shift through derivative values and non-derivative values to get to the fundamental values which everyone holds. Here are the things which are really important to the individual, whose pursuit makes happy and life worth living for. To compromise these values causes great suffering and a loss of direction.

Self-Connectedness

The information to be gained from inside one's body can be tremendous if one is willing to listen to it. We produce a lot of information in our body, which, though it requires the environment to interact with, is in many ways a very complicated self-contained system. The parallel information processing power of the nervous system and the networks of cells of the rest of the body, connected by chemical and electric pathways, is very large. Even information coming in from the outside world has to pass through cellular networks to reach higher brain centers.

Self-connectedness means being aware that the information reaching the brain is made up of information that is largely influenced by the information processed in our bodies. It requires becoming aware of the shear infinity of information sources our brain is processing, and not just the sentence one may see on a computer screen at work. This awareness is important to deal with anxiety, OCD, burnout, depression, psychosis and a host of other conditions. It does not mean one has to process all this information consciously, just that the processes are stable, while the sources and the information may change. Our values as a result of these processes change little, while our experiences on the summer vacation may be vastly different from year to year.

Time

To many patients, time has become convoluted. They do not know what to do with their past, are afraid to think about their feature, and are caught between past and present which deprives them of the present. Making sense of the relationship between the present, the past and the future establishes the bridges that can anchor them in the present moment. Awareness, feelings, feedback and communication are important factors in this process.

Thinking about values and interests helps to rebuild a future, but this might confront the patient with 'bad decisions' in the past. The best way to deal with this is through acceptance and integration. This means the past has to be accepted and to a certain extent embraced, which is an important process in therapy.

Questions

The most important communication tool one has in psychotherapy is to ask questions. In Socratic questioning the question can lead to insights for both, the patient and the therapist. However, to ask questions that bring greater insight requires having a sense of the type of answers that will be useful to allowing the patient greater awareness, insight and connectedness. The type of answers may often not be apparent early in therapy. However, they should be related to greater happiness, and thus a knowledge of the patient's values, interests and aspirations.

Meaningful Communication

One needs to have faith that the interaction between therapist and patient will reveal the information that provides the course in treatment. And this will always happen if there is meaningful communication, which means that something new is communicated every time information travels between the two partners in the interaction. Information can be little gestures or a twitch on the forehand which signal emotions or thought processes, words that can be understood by the other person and in general every signal that can be sent and received by therapist and patient. This requirement is easy to satisfy, if there is a minimal openness to engage in a therapeutic process.

Types of Intervention

An intervention should create greater awareness, insight and connectedness in the patient. A few examples follow.

Questioning

"I want to be in control in social situations."

"What does it mean to be in control in social situations?"

"I would feel free, I would not think anymore so much, I would not analyze so much what other people think."

Questions are really the key tool in any therapeutic work. Although most patients are looking for answers, it is important for the therapist to resist the urge to give quick answers. The best answers come from the patient, because no one has as much information about the patient as the patient herself. Over time, the questions should pursue an objective, namely to help the patient to acquire the skills to see more meaning in himself and the world.

Assembling

The information from the patient needs to be put in a different form to create something new. Often, the easiest way to do this is by way of summary, such as

"So, you are telling me that you ..."

A summary is sufficient if it presents the information from the patient in a novel way. However, the communication from the therapist should also reflect on the communication patterns and styles used between therapist and patient, which is one of the key elements of why the 'talking cure' works. It is not necessarily a reflection on the relationship between therapist and patient, but on how messages are assembled and disassembled, how information is identified as meaningful, and how all this takes place relative to the present situation and the communication space.

"I understand that … It sounds to me that … What do you mean by …?"

The Logic Test

The logical test is a result from assembling the information. Here contradictions can become clear, or spots that have not been thought through. Often, there is a belief that the emotions and the rational mind are at opposing sides. However, when a patient helps to think through things in a constructive way, it often helps to identify and reconnect with underlying emotions. The same also works in the other direction. Emotional energy is important to drive the cognitive processes of the mind. The lack of motivation and initiative one sees in depression is linked to an emotional disconnect and leads to impairments in an individual's ability to drive rational thought processes.

Imagining

Imagining is that step in which people project their wishes, needs and aspirations into their inner world using building blocks they know from the real world. It is here where we build the world we compare the real world with. This comparison motivates us to change our world, but it can also raise emotions, such as fear or happiness. As emotions have influence over the worlds we imagine, so the worlds we imagine have influence over our emotions.

Our vision of the future plays an especially important role, because it can provide motivation and a sense of direction, as long as it is congruent with the person's underlying values, aspirations and interests.

"Can you imagine what it would be like not to feel socially anxious anymore?"

Imagination is not used to disappear from the real world, but as a means to find new answers and creative solutions in the real world. It is thus important to see the imagination as another tool to help achieve health, happiness and fulfil own needs and aspirations in the shared world.

Bridging Imagination and Shared World

The focus needs to be on changes that may have to be made in the present world to get closer to the imagined world. These thoughts should then lead to behavior changes that get the patient closer to where she wants to be. It is thus a patient's discovery of and connection with own values, needs and aspiration which facilitate the bridge between the imagined and the shared world, because they should be equivalent and relevant in both spheres.

Creating new communication pattern

Change also means one has to communicate with the world in new ways. This grows out of the rediscovered values and interests, the feedback and dynamics in the work with the therapist and the life of the patient outside the therapy. Over time, the new communication patterns should solidify as the patient is reinforced by better interactions with the environment.

If a communication pattern or a communication process helps the patient connect with or achieve the authentic self in the form of deeply held values, interests and aspirations, then it is adaptive to implement it and to use it more often, either generally or limited to specific circumstances.

Communication patterns and styles are practiced and experimented with in the interaction between therapist and patient. Therefore, it is important that the communication setting is one where the patient can feel safe in, safe enough to experiment without having to feel anxious about the therapist's judgment of him and without any fear of recriminations.

Keeping the Interaction Alive

Important is to keep the interaction going, because the exchange of information in the form of meaningful messages is the process where insight can be gained, and change occur. This requires a commitment of therapist and patient to continue engaging in the free flow of information which is necessary so that a wide spectrum of meaningful messages can be communicated.

Conclusion

Psychotherapy is both, creative and supportive work. It requires a keen eye for the process and the dynamics unfolding within a session. Working with the patient on communication patterns, interaction dynamics, uncovering values and basic interests often goes a long way towards a successful therapy.

References

Haverkampf, C. J. (2017a). A Case of Severe ADHD. *J Psychiatry Psychotherapy Communication, 6*(2), 31–36.

Haverkampf, C. J. (2017b). *ADHD and Psychotherapy (2)*. Retrieved from http://www.jonathanhaverkampf.com/

Haverkampf, C. J. (2017c). CBT and Psychodynamic Psychotherapy - A Comparison. *J Psychiatry Psychotherapy Communication, 6*(2), 61–68.

Haverkampf, C. J. (2017d). *Communication-Focused Therapy (CFT)* (2nd ed.). Dublin: Psychiatry Psychotherapy Communication Publishing Ltd.

Haverkampf, C. J. (2017e). Communication-Focused Therapy (CFT) for ADHD. *J Psychiatry Psychotherapy Communication, 6*(4), 110–115.

Haverkampf, C. J. (2017f). Treatment-Resistant Adult ADHD. *J Psychiatry Psychotherapy Communication, 6*(1), 18–26.

Haverkampf, C. J. (2018). *An Overview of Psychiatric Medication* (3rd ed.). Dublin: Psychiatry Psychotherapy Communication Publishing Ltd.